MICROSOFT WORD QUICK START 2024 GUIDE

JEXONIA GRANEER

INTRODUCTION

Embracing the Power of Word Processing

In the ever-evolving landscape of digital technology, the ability to communicate effectively and efficiently is paramount. The "Microsoft Word Quick Start 2024 Guide" stands as a beacon, illuminating the path for individuals navigating the intricate corridors of Microsoft Word 2024. This introduction lays the foundation for a transformative journey from novice to proficient user of one of the world's most renowned word processing tools.

The Evolution of Word Processing

The inception of word processing marked a revolutionary shift in how we approach writing and document creation. From the rudimentary typewriters to the sophisticated software of today, each iteration has strived to enhance user experience and capability. Microsoft Word, a frontrunner in this evolution, has consistently set benchmarks for innovation, ease of use, and functionality.

Microsoft Word 2024: A New Horizon

Microsoft Word 2024 emerges as a culmination of decades of refinement. This version, more than any before, is tailored to the demands of the modern user – balancing simplicity with advanced features. It caters to a wide array of needs, from crafting a simple letter to designing complex reports, making it an indispensable tool for students, professionals, and hobbyists alike.

What Sets Microsoft Word 2024 Apart

Enhanced User Interface: Microsoft Word 2024 debuts an intuitive, user-friendly interface. This design not only eases the learning curve for new users but also streamlines the process for seasoned veterans.

Robust Feature Set: The software boasts a comprehensive array of features, including advanced editing tools, collaborative functions, and customizable templates, all designed to boost productivity and creativity.

Cross-Platform Compatibility: In an era where work and personal life blend across multiple devices, Microsoft Word 2024's cross-platform compatibility ensures seamless transition and access, regardless of the device in use.

Cloud Integration and Collaboration: The integration with cloud services facilitates real-time collaboration and document sharing, making remote work and team projects more efficient than ever.

The Purpose of This Guide

The "Microsoft Word Quick Start 2024 Guide" is tailored to unlock the full potential of Microsoft Word 2024 for its users. Whether you are a first-time user or looking to upgrade your skills with the latest features, this guide serves as your comprehensive manual. The chapters are meticulously structured to walk you through every aspect of the program – from basic operations to advanced functionalities.

Chapter Overview

Getting Started with Microsoft Word: This chapter introduces the basics of Word 2024, covering everything from obtaining and installing the software to creating your first document.

Introduction to the Interface and Core Functions: Here, you'll familiarize yourself with the user interface, learn about the Ribbon, the status bar, and start configuring Word to suit your preferences.

Mastering Document Creation: Dive into the practical aspects of document creation, learning about input devices, typing techniques, and essential keyboard shortcuts.

Advanced Editing Techniques: Elevate your editing skills with advanced techniques, including managing paragraphs, understanding line breaks, and utilizing the undo and redo commands.

Enhancing Document Presentation: This chapter focuses on enhancing the visual appeal of your documents, covering styles, themes, headers, footers, and more.

Organizing Complex Content: Learn how to effectively manage complex documents, including working with tables, graphical elements, and formatting options.

Document Management and Collaboration: Explore the features that make Word 2024 a powerful tool for collaboration, including document sharing, security features, and recovery options.

Streamlining Your Workflow: Discover tips and tricks to make your work in Word more efficient.

Keyboard Shortcuts in Word: A comprehensive guide to keyboard shortcuts that will speed up your workflow and increase efficiency.

Navigating the World of Microsoft Word 2024

As we delve deeper into the "Microsoft Word Quick Start 2024 Guide," it's essential to appreciate the nuances that make Word 2024 not just a tool, but a companion in your digital journey. This introduction serves as a portal, offering a glimpse into the myriad ways Word 2024 can enhance your writing, organization, and presentation skills.

The Essence of Word Processing in the Modern Era

In a world increasingly reliant on digital communication, Word 2024 stands as a testament to the evolution of word processing. It embodies the fusion of simplicity and complexity, making it accessible to the novice while still offering depth for the power user. This duality is the cornerstone of Word 2024, providing a platform that adapts to your individual needs and growth.

The Intuitive Interface: A Gateway to Creativity

The interface of Microsoft Word 2024 is a masterclass in design efficiency. Every element, from the Ribbon to the Quick Access Toolbar, is strategically placed to enhance usability. The minimalist design ensures that tools are readily available without overwhelming the user, creating a workspace that encourages focus and creativity.

Customization: Tailoring Word to Your Needs

One of the hallmarks of Word 2024 is its customization capabilities. This guide will show you how to tailor the interface to match your workflow, whether you prefer a clean, distraction-free environment or a tool-laden workspace for quick access to advanced features. Customization extends beyond the interface; you'll learn to personalize settings, templates, and even the autocorrect dictionary to make Word truly your own.

The Power of Collaboration and Connectivity

Collaboration and connectivity are at the heart of Word 2024's functionality. With cloud integration, you can work on documents from anywhere, on any device, ensuring that your work is always within reach. This guide will explore the collaborative features of Word 2024, including real-time editing, commenting, and sharing options that make teamwork seamless and efficient.

Security and Document Management: A Priority

In an age where data security is paramount, Word 2024 offers robust options to protect your documents. From password protection to advanced encryption, this guide will navigate you through setting up security measures to safeguard your sensitive information. Additionally, we'll delve into efficient document management techniques, ensuring that your work is organized, accessible, and secure.

Beyond Text: The Visual Aspect of Documents

Word 2024 transcends beyond mere text editing. It offers a wide array of tools for adding and manipulating graphical elements, creating visually stunning documents. Whether you're inserting images, crafting custom charts, or designing intricate layouts, Word 2024 empowers you to bring visual flair to your work. This guide will provide step-by-step instructions to master these visual tools, helping you to convey your message not just through words but through impactful design.

Accessibility: Making Word Work for Everyone

Microsoft's commitment to accessibility is evident in Word 2024. Features like Read Aloud, Accessibility Checker, and support for screen readers ensure that the software is usable for everyone, regardless of ability. This guide will cover these accessibility features in depth, ensuring that Word 2024 is an inclusive tool for all users.

Conclusion: The Journey Begins

As we wrap up this introduction, it's important to remember that this guide is more than just a manual; it's a journey through the capabilities of Microsoft Word 2024. Each chapter is designed to build upon the last, gradually enhancing your proficiency and confidence in using this powerful tool. The "Microsoft Word Quick Start 2024 Guide" is your key to unlocking the full potential of Word 2024, and this introduction is just the first step on a path to becoming an accomplished and efficient Word user. Welcome to a journey of discovery, empowerment, and mastery in the world of Microsoft Word 2024.

As we embark on this journey together, the "Microsoft Word Quick Start 2024 Guide" aims not only to educate but also to inspire. The power of Microsoft Word 2024 lies not just in its features but in how you, the user, harness them to bring your ideas to life. This introduction is just the beginning. The pages that follow are your roadmap to mastering Microsoft Word 2024, paving the way for you to transform your thoughts into impactful, well-crafted documents. Welcome to a world of endless possibilities with Microsoft Word 2024.

CONTENTS

CHAPTER 1. GETTING STARTED WITH MICROSOFT WORD

1.1 Understanding the Basics of Microsoft Word 2024 – What Is a Word Processor?

In the digital era, the ability to create, edit, and manage documents is indispensable, and Microsoft Word 2024 stands as a testament to how far word processing technology has come. Before delving into the myriad features of this sophisticated software, let's take a step back and understand the foundational element of Word — what exactly a word processor is.

A word processor is a software application used for the production of any sort of printable material. It's an electronic device or computer software application that performs the task of composing, editing, formatting, and sometimes printing text. In simpler terms, it's your digital typewriter, packed with features that make it possible to create complex and beautifully formatted documents with ease.

Microsoft Word 2024 is the latest iteration in a long line of word processing software from Microsoft. It's part of the broader suite of productivity applications known as Microsoft Office, which also includes programs like Excel and PowerPoint. Over the years, Word has evolved from a simple text editor to a powerful tool capable of handling everything from basic letter writing to the creation of complex reports and interactive digital documents.

The evolution of word processors mirrors the advancements in computing technology. Initially, word processors were standalone machines, which then transitioned into software applications with the advent of personal computing. Now, they are often part of cloud-based systems, enabling users to access their documents from any device with internet connectivity.

Microsoft Word 2024 incorporates the traditional functionality of word processing with the latest advancements in software design and user experience. Its intuitive interface allows users, whether beginners or advanced, to perform tasks with straightforward commands and minimal learning curve.

Understanding the layout of Microsoft Word 2024 is crucial. When you open Word, you are greeted with the Start Screen — this is where your word processing journey begins. The Start Screen offers quick access to a range of templates and recent documents, as well as the option to start a new blank document. Once you select or open a document, you'll be introduced to the primary workspace.

The workspace consists of a blank page by default, a blinking cursor awaiting your input. This is your canvas, where text, images, and other multimedia can be inserted and arranged. The top portion of the window hosts the Ribbon, which is essentially the control panel of Word, housing a plethora of tools divided into tabs like 'Home', 'Insert', 'Design', 'Layout', and more.

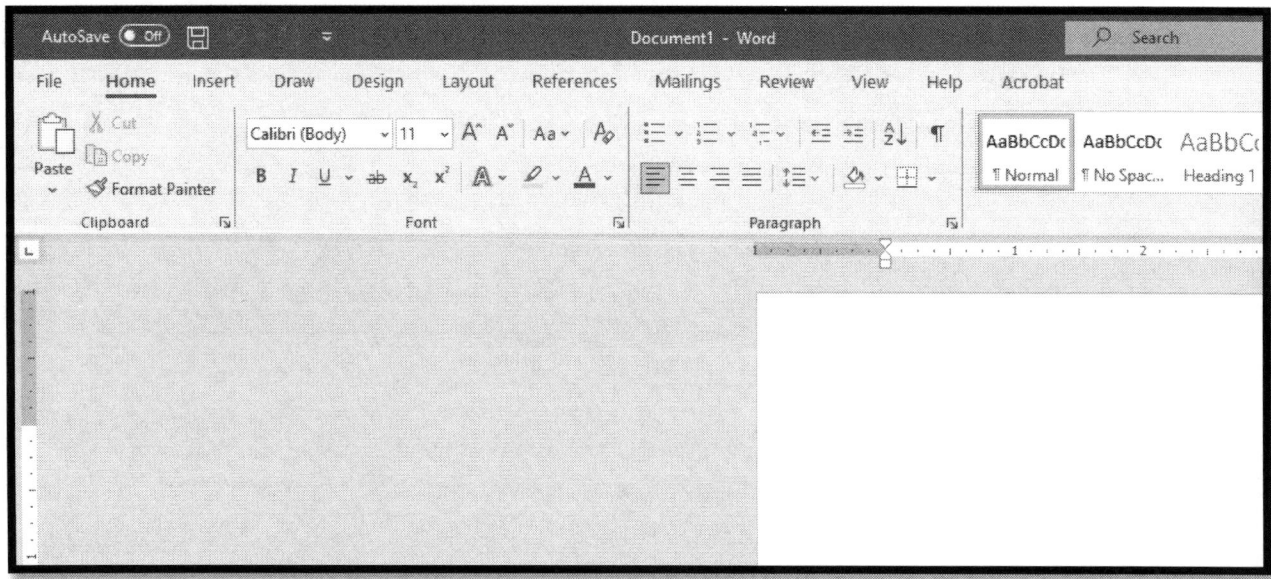

The 'Home' tab is often where most of the basic text formatting tools are found, such as font style and size, text alignment, and bullet points. As you progress, the 'Insert' tab allows you to add pictures, charts, links, and other non-text elements into your document. The 'Design' and 'Layout' tabs offer options to modify the overall appearance and structure of the entire document.

Microsoft Word 2024 also introduces some smart features like 'Researcher' and 'Editor'. 'Researcher' helps you find reliable sources and content relevant to your topic right within Word, while 'Editor' is an advanced proofing tool that not only checks spelling and grammar but also suggests stylistic improvements.

One of the remarkable qualities of Microsoft Word is its versatility. It's used by students for crafting essays, business professionals for creating reports and memos, authors for writing manuscripts, and even graphic designers for constructing brochures and flyers. Its broad applicability across professions is a testament to its flexibility and depth of functionality.

Collaboration is a cornerstone of Microsoft Word 2024, acknowledging the modern need for teamwork and cooperative editing. With features like real-time co-authoring, comments, and track changes, multiple people can work on the same document simultaneously, no matter where they are in the world.

In conclusion, Microsoft Word 2024 is more than just a word processor — it's a comprehensive tool that caters to the creation and management of written content. Whether you're typing up a simple note or compiling an extensive report, Word provides the functionality and ease of use that have made it the industry standard. For beginners, it starts with recognizing the power at your fingertips: a software that encapsulates the collective progress of digital writing technology, designed to accommodate the ever-growing and diverse demands of users worldwide.

1.2 How to Obtain Microsoft Word 2024 – Buying or Subscription Options

In the landscape of digital word processing, Microsoft Word 2024 is a giant whose features are as expansive as its user base. But before one can harness its capabilities, it must first be acquired. This raises the pivotal question: How does one obtain Microsoft Word 2024? Today, Microsoft offers various avenues to access this essential piece of software, ranging from one-time purchases to subscription models.

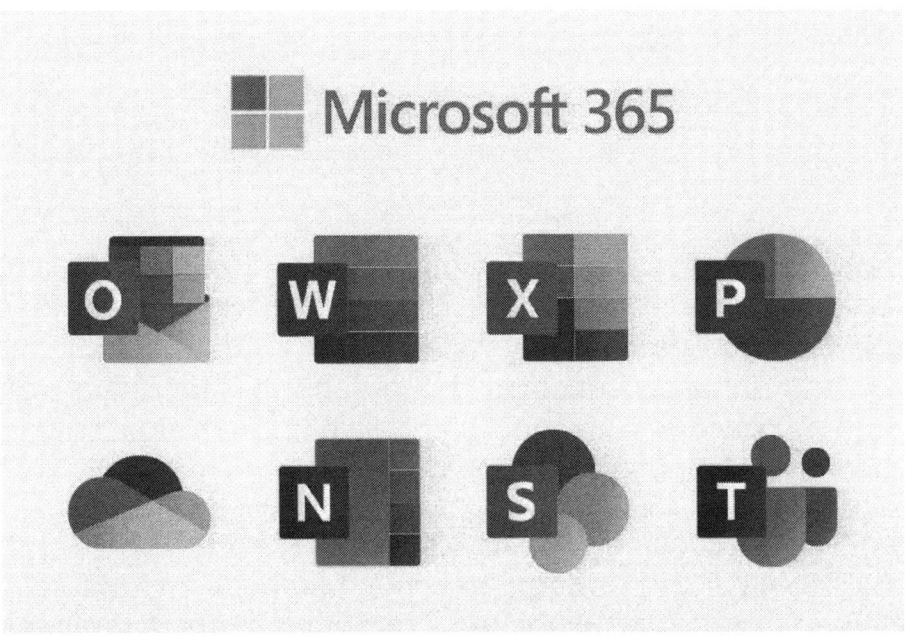

The traditional approach to software acquisition was a one-time purchase, and Microsoft Word was no exception. You would buy a physical copy of the software, receive a product key, install the program, and it was yours indefinitely. With the introduction of cloud computing and the evolution of Microsoft's business model, the company has shifted toward a subscription service known as Microsoft 365.

Microsoft 365 Subscription

The subscription service is a comprehensive package that not only includes Microsoft Word but also other staple applications like Excel, PowerPoint, and depending on the plan you choose, a suite of additional software and services. Microsoft 365 comes in various tiers, catering to different needs and budgets. There are personal plans, family plans (which cover multiple users, typically up to six), and a range of business plans offering additional services geared towards collaboration and enterprise management.

Microsoft Office 365 Personal Pricing

	Office 365 Personal	Office 365 Home
Monthly price	$5.83	$8.33
Number of users	1	6
Products	Word, Excel, PowerPoint, Outlook, Publisher, Access	Word, Excel, PowerPoint, Outlook, Publisher, Access
OneDrive Storage	1 TB	1 TB per user
Skype Minutes	60 minutes per month	60 minutes per month per person

A major benefit of the Microsoft 365 subscription is that it guarantees you always have the most up-to-date version of Word. With Microsoft Word 2024, as with its predecessors, updates are regularly rolled out to improve functionality, introduce new features, and enhance security. This means that the initial version of Word 2024 you start with will evolve over time, gaining new capabilities and staying abreast of the latest computing standards.

Another compelling aspect of subscribing is the integration of cloud services. Microsoft 365 heavily incorporates OneDrive, Microsoft's cloud storage platform, which provides a seamless experience for storing documents and accessing them from any device with an internet connection. This connectivity also facilitates collaboration, allowing for multiple users to work on a document simultaneously.

One-Time Purchase

For those who prefer owning their software outright without ongoing costs, Microsoft still offers a standalone version of Microsoft Word. This is typically branded as "Office 2024 Home & Student" or "Office 2024 Professional". The one-time purchase grants you a perpetual license to the software, meaning you pay once and own it forever. However, unlike the subscription service, this option does not include the regular updates that add features and improvements. Security updates are included for a limited time, but eventually, even these will cease, and the software will become outdated.

Educational Licensing

Students and educators may have special options to obtain Microsoft Word 2024 at significantly reduced prices or even for free. Educational institutions often have agreements with Microsoft that allow them to provide Office software to their students and faculty as part of their enrollment or employment. If you are a student, teacher, or faculty member, it's worth checking if your institution participates in this program.

Trial Version

If you're unsure about which option is right for you, Microsoft typically offers a trial version of Microsoft 365. This trial provides full access to the suite of Office applications for a limited period, often one month. This is an excellent opportunity to explore the full range of capabilities of Microsoft Word 2024 without any upfront commitment.

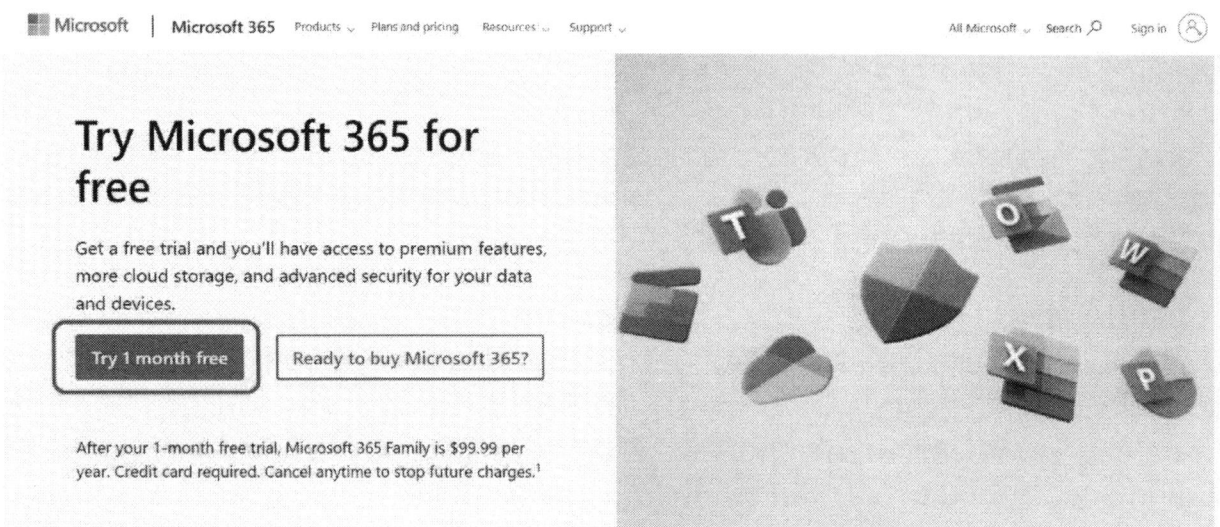

Purchasing Platforms

Microsoft Word 2024 can be purchased directly from the Microsoft website, which is the most straightforward method. Alternatively, licensed digital product retailers offer Microsoft Office products, sometimes at discounted rates. Physical copies can still be found at electronics stores, although these are becoming less common with the rise of digital distribution.

Things to Consider

When deciding which purchasing option is best for you, consider your specific needs. If you require Word for basic document creation, the standalone version might suffice. However, if you are looking to utilize the full potential of Word with regular updates, cloud storage, and collaboration tools, the subscription service would be the optimal choice.

The collaborative and ever-evolving nature of work and education suggests that a subscription service could offer the most value in the long term. It's also worth noting that as software moves increasingly towards service-based models, subscription options may offer more than just software—they often include a level of technical support, exclusive features, and integration with other services that standalone versions do not.

In summary, obtaining Microsoft Word 2024 is a decision that hinges on your use case, preference for ownership versus access, and how integral the software's advanced features are to your daily operations. The transition from ownership to subscription reflects a broader shift in software delivery, emphasizing continuous improvement, integration, and collaboration. Regardless of which path you choose, Word 2024 stands ready to assist in transforming your thoughts into text, your ideas into documents, and your visions into realities.

1.3. Installing Microsoft Word 2024 – A Step-by-Step Guide

Installing Microsoft Word 2024 is a straightforward process that can be accomplished in a few simple steps. Whether you have opted for a Microsoft 365 subscription, a one-time purchase of Office 2024, or have access through an educational institution, setting up Word on your device is designed to be user-friendly and quick. In this guide, we'll walk you through the installation process step by step.

Pre-Installation Checklist

Before you begin the installation process, ensure that your computer meets the minimum system requirements for Microsoft Word 2024. These typically include a compatible operating system like Windows 10 or 11, a certain amount of RAM, and available disk space. You should also have a stable internet connection to download the software and perform updates.

Processor	Memory (RAM)	Hard Disk	Display
1.6 GHz or faster, 2-core processor	4 GB RAM for 64-bit; 2 GB RAM for 32-bit Graphics hardware acceleration requires DirectX 9 or later, with WDDM 2.0 or higher for Windows 10	4GB free disk space	1280 x 768 or higher screen resolution

Step 1: Purchasing or Subscribing

Depending on your chosen method of acquisition, the first step is either purchasing Microsoft Word 2024 or subscribing to Microsoft 365. If you're purchasing a one-time copy, you might receive a product key in a retail box or via email. For Microsoft 365 subscribers, your Microsoft account will be your key to access Word 2024.

Step 2: Sign in to Your Microsoft Account

Visit the Microsoft website and sign into your Microsoft account. If you haven't created an account yet, you'll need to sign up for one. This account is crucial as it will be used to manage your subscription or register your one-time purchase.

Step 3: Redeem Your Product Key (If Applicable)

If you have a product key from a one-time purchase, you will need to redeem it. Once logged into your account, navigate to the "Services & subscriptions" tab, and then select "Redeem a code or gift card". Enter your 25-character product key without the dashes. After entering your key, the product associated with it will be added to your account and ready for download.

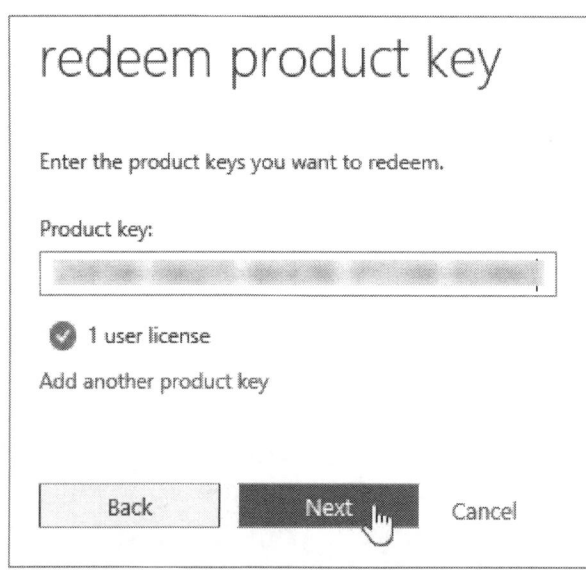

Step 4: Begin the Installation

With Microsoft 365, you don't need a product key. Simply go to the "Services & subscriptions" section, where you should see Microsoft Word 2024 included in your list of subscriptions. Here, you will find an option to "Install Office," which you should click to begin the download process. For a one-time purchase, after redeeming your product key, you should also see the option to "Install Office."

Step 5: Download Microsoft Word 2024

Clicking the "Install Office" button will initiate the download of the installation file. If prompted, choose the version (32-bit or 64-bit) that matches your system's architecture, and then start the download. The file size can be significant, so the download time will depend on your internet speed.

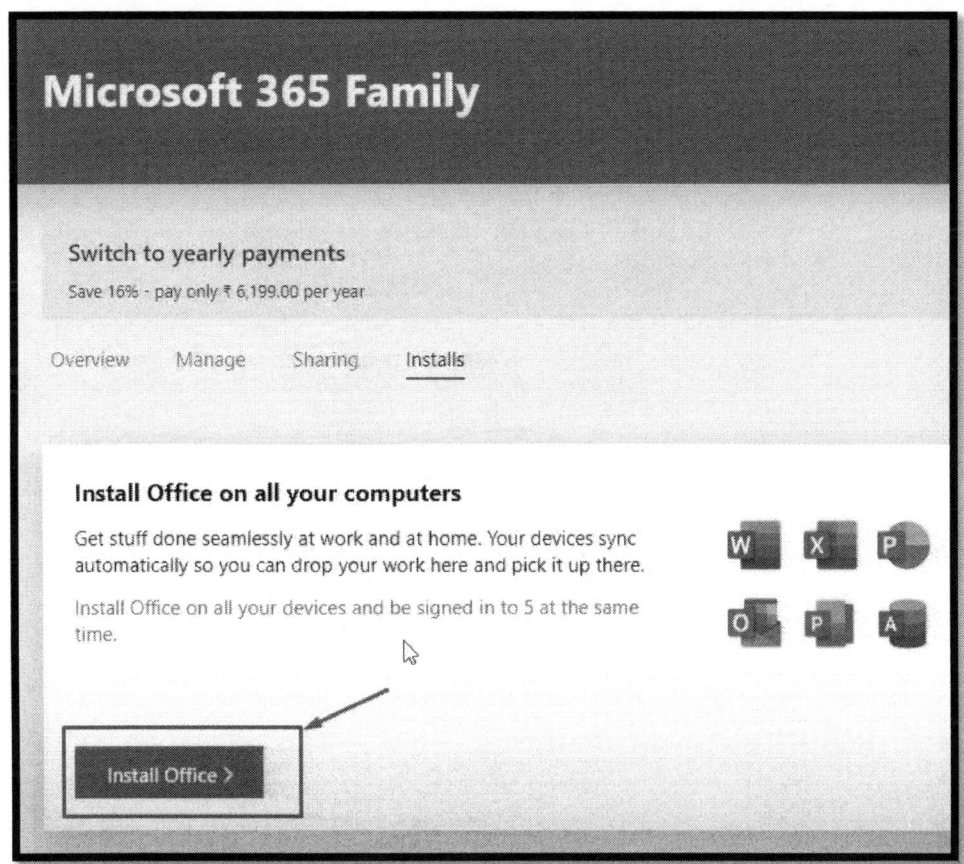

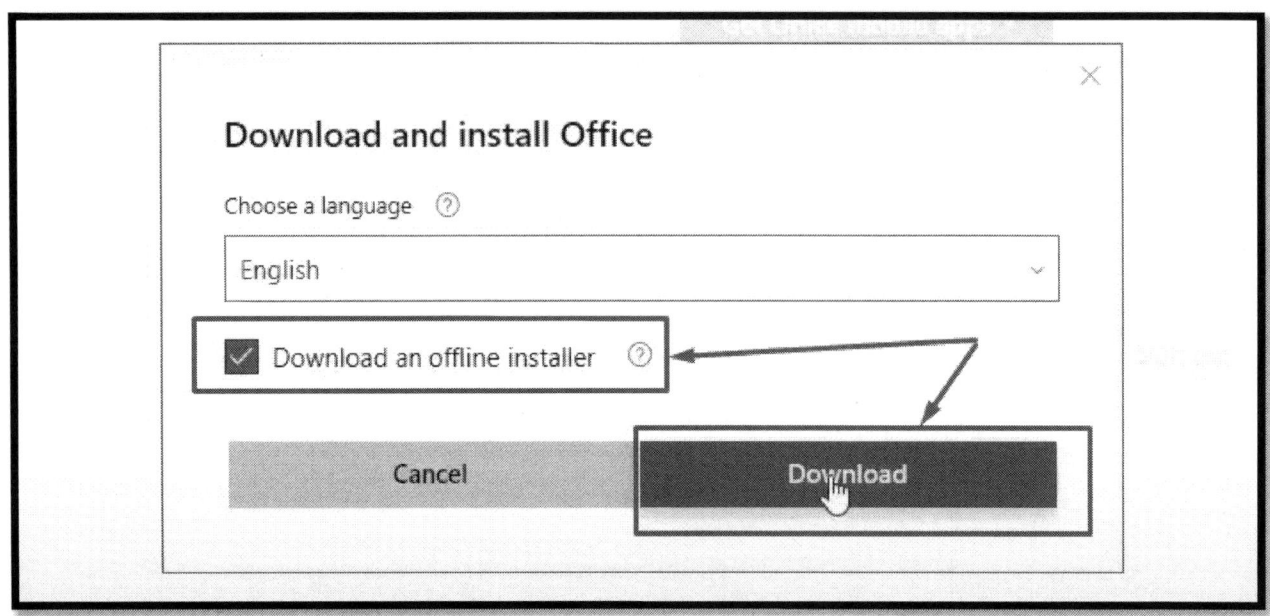

Step 6: Run the Installation File

Once the download is complete, locate the installation file, which is usually in the Downloads folder, unless you specified another location. Double-click the file to run the installer. On Windows, you may receive a User Account Control prompt asking for permission to allow the app to make changes to your device; click "Yes" to continue.

Step 7: Follow the Installation Prompts

The installer will take over from here, and you will see a window showing the installation progress. It might take a few minutes to install all the necessary components of Microsoft Word 2024. During this process, you can continue using your computer, but it might run a bit slower than usual.

Step 8: Installation Completion

Once the installation is complete, you will receive a message indicating that Microsoft Word 2024 is installed on your device. You can then open the software by clicking "Close" on the installation complete notification, navigating to the Start menu on your computer, and finding Word listed there.

Step 9: Activation

When you launch Microsoft Word for the first time, you may be prompted to activate the product. If you're a Microsoft 365 subscriber, ensure you're signed in with your Microsoft account that has the subscription. For one-time purchases, the product key you redeemed should automatically activate Word 2024.

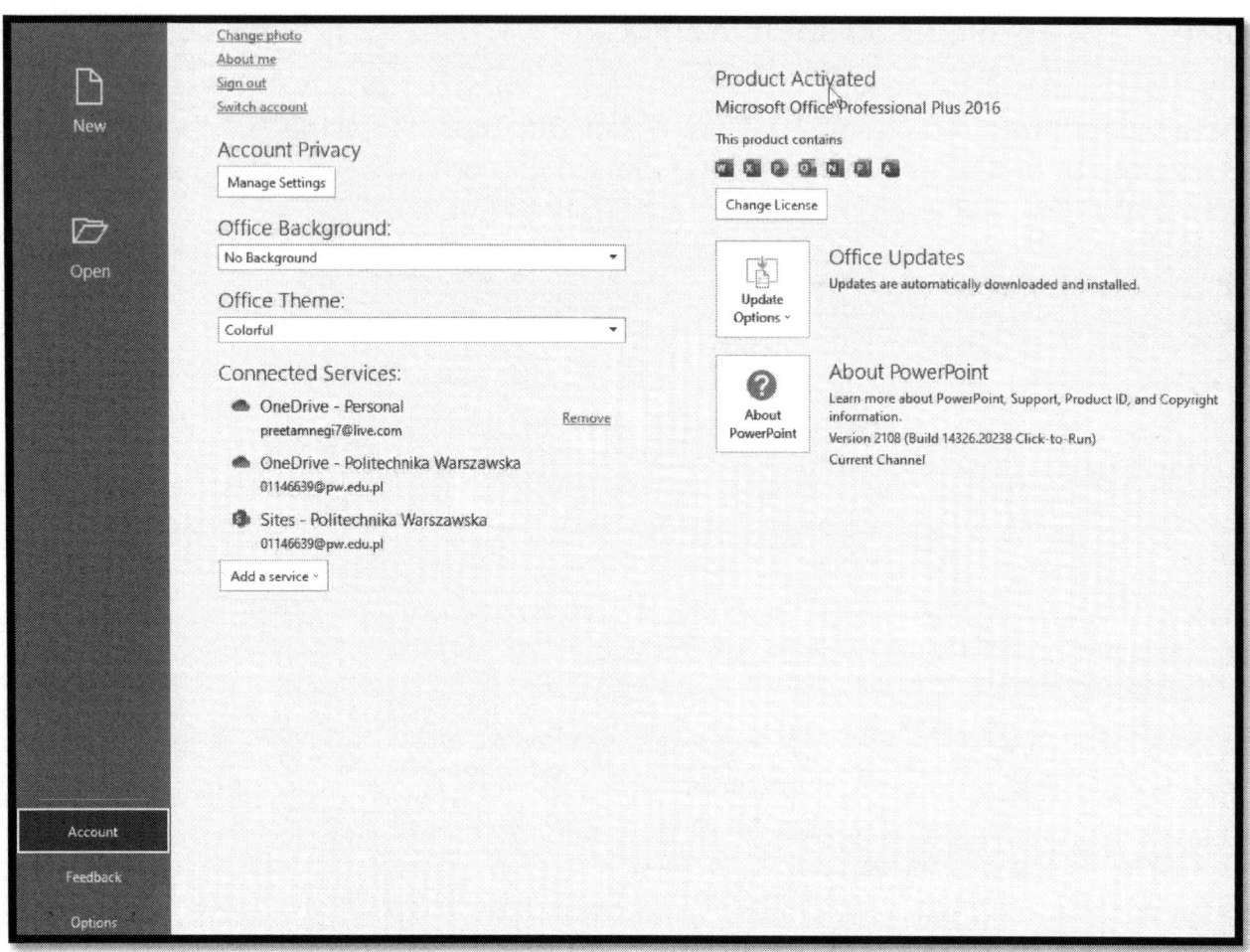

Step 10: Update and Customize

After the installation and activation, it is a good practice to check for updates. Microsoft regularly releases patches and features updates. In Word, click on "File," then "Account," and select "Update Options." Choose "Update Now" to ensure you have the latest version. Additionally, you can customize Word settings to suit your preferences.

And with that, Microsoft Word 2024 is installed and ready for use. The installation process is designed to be hassle-free, but if you encounter any issues, Microsoft provides detailed support documentation and customer service to assist you.
Now you can begin exploring the innovative features and tools that Word 2024 offers, taking your document creation and word processing to new heights.

1.4. Opening Microsoft Word for the First Time – Navigating the Start Screen

The first launch of Microsoft Word 2024 is not just an introduction to a robust word processing tool; it's the beginning of a journey where creativity and functionality meet. As a novice user, the Start Screen can be both inviting and overwhelming with its myriad of options and settings. This guide is tailored to help you navigate the Start Screen with ease, ensuring your first experience with Word is as seamless and productive as possible.

Welcome to Word 2024

Upon opening Microsoft Word 2024 for the first time, you'll be greeted by the Start Screen—a hub from where you can access everything Word has to offer. The Start Screen is designed with simplicity and intuition in mind, allowing users to jump straight into document creation or to explore the Word environment.

1. The Layout

The Start Screen is neatly divided into several sections. On the left-hand side, you'll find a sidebar that includes a list of recent documents, which makes it easy to pick up where you left off. Below the recent documents, there's an option to open other files stored on your computer or cloud storage.

2. Starting a New Document

In the center of the Start Screen is the 'New' section. Here, you can choose to start a blank document or browse a selection of templates. Templates are pre-designed documents for a variety of purposes, from business letters to brochures, that can give you a head start on your project.

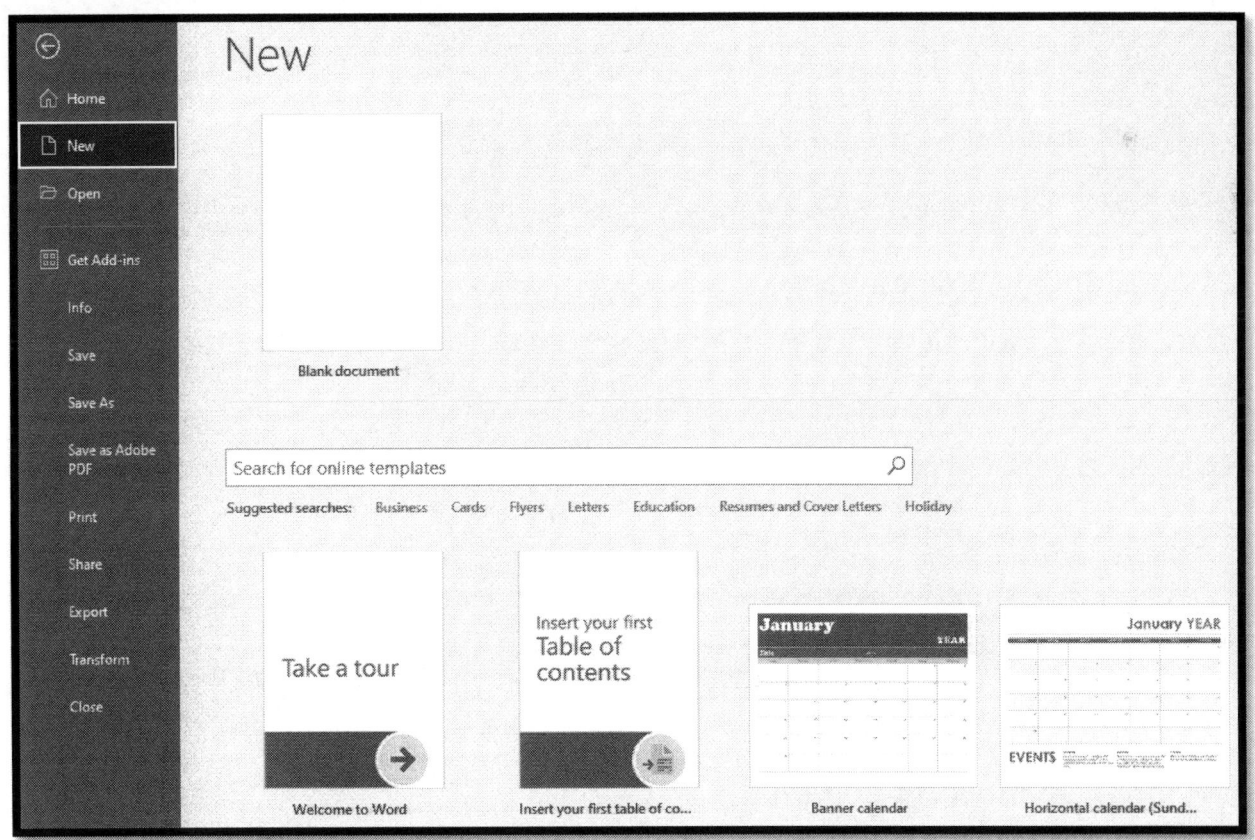

3. Templates Galore

Word 2024's templates are more than just a starting point—they are learning tools. Hovering over a template will give you a quick preview and often includes tips on when and how to use it. Selecting a template will open a new document with placeholder text and formatted design elements, which you can then customize.

4. The Account and Options Area

On the right side of the Start Screen, you may find an area dedicated to your Microsoft account information. This is where you can sign in with your Microsoft account, switch accounts, or sign out. Below your account information, there's usually a small gear icon, which opens the Word Options dialog box where you can change Word's default settings.

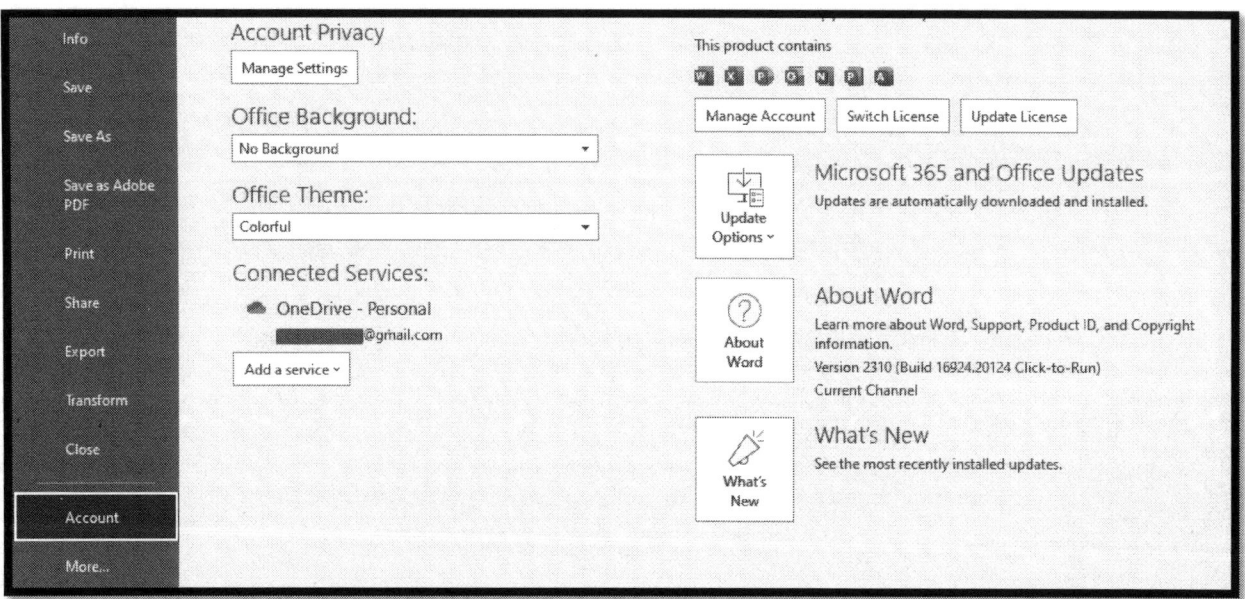

5. Learning and Assistance

Word 2024's Start Screen also features an area dedicated to learning resources. Here, you can access tutorials, helpful tips, and guidance on how to use various features within Word. This is an excellent place for beginners to become acquainted with the capabilities of the software.

6. Search Bar Functionality

Prominently featured at the top is a search bar. The search functionality in Word 2024 goes beyond finding templates; it allows you to search for commands, help articles, and even content within your documents, making it a powerful tool for new users.

7. Recent Documents and Pinned Files

As you start working with Word 2024, the documents you've opened or edited recently will populate the 'Recent' list, allowing for easy access. A useful feature is the ability to pin documents that you frequently work on to the top of this list, ensuring they're always readily available.

8. Accessing Word Settings

For more advanced settings, there is usually an 'Options' or 'Settings' button located towards the bottom or within the menu. This is where you can customize Word's behavior to your liking, from changing the default font and size to adjusting the proofing settings.

9. Accessibility Features

Microsoft has always prioritized accessibility, and Word 2024 is no exception. On the Start Screen, you can locate and enable various accessibility features to tailor your experience to any specific needs you might have.

10. Familiarizing with the Interface

Take a moment to click through different tabs and icons to familiarize yourself with where everything is located. Don't worry about changing anything irreversibly—Word 2024 is designed to be a safe environment to explore and learn.

1.5. Creating Your First Document – Overview of Key Features

Stepping into the realm of Microsoft Word 2024, your first act of creation—crafting a new document—is both an initiation and a revelation of the program's capabilities. This foundational step is your gateway to exploring an array of features designed to enhance the functionality and aesthetics of your work.

When you select 'New Document,' you are greeted with a blank page that whispers the promise of infinite possibilities. This canvas is where text, images, and ideas converge, facilitated by an intuitive set of tools and functions. Key features at your disposal include the 'Ribbon'—Word's command hub—that houses tabs with grouped tools for inserting elements, layout adjustments, and reviewing your work for that professional touch.

Styles and formatting options allow you to define the appearance of text with just a click, setting the tone and visual appeal. Meanwhile, the 'Design' tab offers themes and style sets, adding sophistication to your document without the need for complex graphic design skills.

Your first creation is also a learning experience, one where 'Undo' and 'Redo' buttons become valuable allies as you experiment and refine. Whether it's a letter, a report, or an invitation, Microsoft Word 2024's key features empower you to bring your vision to paper, or screen, with clarity and ease.

CHAPTER 2. INTRODUCTION TO THE INTERFACE AND CORE FUNCTIONS

2.1. Familiarizing with the User Interface – Components of Microsoft Word 2024

When you step into the realm of Microsoft Word 2024, you're not just dealing with a blank page waiting for words; you're engaging with a sophisticated platform equipped with a multitude of tools designed to make document creation a seamless experience. Understanding the interface is crucial for harnessing the full potential of this powerful word processor. Let's break down the key components of the Microsoft Word 2024 user interface to help you navigate with confidence.

1. The Ribbon

The Ribbon is the control center of Word 2024, a strip that houses all the tools and functions, organized into tabs like Home, Insert, Design, Layout, References, and Review. Each tab is dedicated to a particular aspect of document creation and editing. For example, the 'Home' tab provides quick access to formatting tools, while 'Insert' allows you to add various elements like tables, pictures, or charts to your document. The Ribbon's intuitive layout means that relevant tools are grouped together, streamlining your workflow.

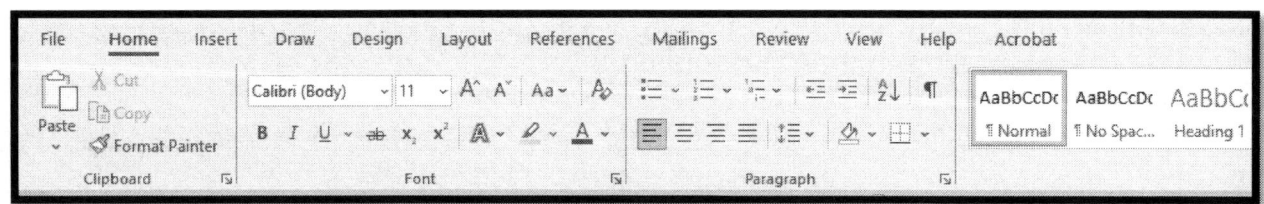

2. The Quick Access Toolbar

Located above the Ribbon, the Quick Access Toolbar is a customizable toolbar where you can pin your most-used commands for easy access, no matter which tab you're on. You can add or remove commands according to your preference, ensuring that the tools you need are always at your fingertips.

3. The Backstage View

Accessed via the 'File' tab, the Backstage View is where the behind-the-scenes magic happens. It's your go-to for all document management tasks, such as saving, opening, printing, and sharing documents. It's also where you can adjust Word's options and account settings.

4. The Document Area

The central and largest part of the interface is the Document Area. This is where your text lives and breathes. You can switch between different views for your document, like 'Print Layout,' 'Web Layout,' or 'Read Mode,' depending on your task at hand. These views can help you understand how your document will look in its final form.

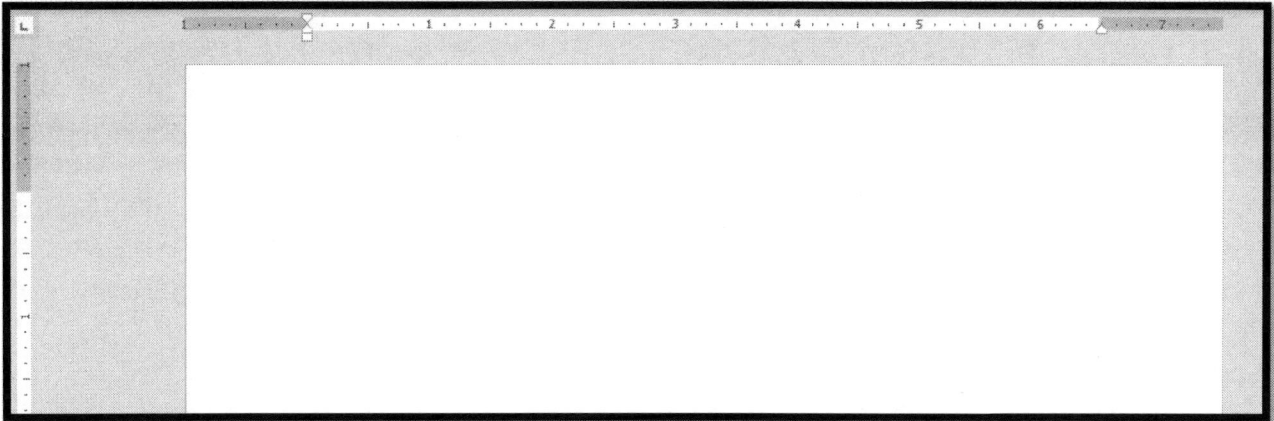

5. The Status Bar

At the very bottom lies the Status Bar, which provides important information about your document at a glance. It shows the page number you're on, word count, and even the language setting. It can also be customized to display additional information like section number, page view options, and zoom controls.

6. The Navigation Pane

The Navigation Pane is a multipurpose tool that helps you quickly move around your document. It can be especially useful for long documents, as it allows you to jump between headings, pages, or search results. This pane is an organizational powerhouse for your document's structure.

7. The Tell Me Bar

A newer addition is the 'Tell Me' bar, a type of intelligent search bar that not only finds commands and tools but also offers help and advice on using them. If you're ever stuck, typing into the 'Tell Me' bar can guide you through the process of what you're trying to achieve.

8. Contextual Menus and Tooltips

Right-clicking on elements within your document brings up contextual menus, offering quick access to relevant commands for the selected object. Hovering over any button or feature in Word brings up tooltips—small, helpful descriptions that explain what each feature does.

2.2. The Ribbon – Accessing Word's Comprehensive Toolset

The Ribbon in Microsoft Word 2024 is the nerve center of the application—a sleek, user-friendly interface that offers a comprehensive toolset at your fingertips. It's where efficiency meets intuition, and functionality meets innovation.

Spanning the top of your document window, the Ribbon is thoughtfully segmented into tabs such as 'Home,' 'Insert,' 'Design,' 'Layout,' 'References,' 'Review,' and 'View.' Each tab is organized into groups that bring related tools together, simplifying the task of formatting, editing, and enhancing your document.

Under the 'Home' tab, you'll find basic formatting tools that allow you to adjust font styles, sizes, and colors, as well as implement bold, italics, underlining, and text alignment. The 'Insert' tab opens a world where you can add tables, pictures, shapes, charts, and hyperlinks, enriching your document's content. Moving over to 'Design,' you're equipped to give your document a cohesive look with themes and style sets. 'Layout' is where you'll control margins, spacing, and orientation, defining the structure of your page.

The Ribbon's intuitive design is customizable, meaning you can pin your most-used tools for quick access, ensuring a smoother workflow. Whether you're drafting your first letter or compiling a complex report, the Ribbon in Microsoft Word 2024 is your launchpad for creating documents that resonate with professionalism and creativity.

2.3. The Status Bar – Keeping Track of Your Document Status

The Status Bar in Microsoft Word 2024 is an essential, albeit often understated, feature nestled at the bottom of the Word window. It serves as your informational dashboard, offering a real-time glimpse into the vital statistics and status of your active document.

This slender bar is a powerhouse of insights—it displays page count, word count, and even character count, indispensable metrics for writers adhering to specific length criteria. As you type and edit, the Status Bar dynamically updates these figures, ensuring you have precise control over your document's length and complexity.

Moreover, the Status Bar indicates the document's proofing status, signaling the presence of grammatical errors or misspellings that need your attention—critical for maintaining professionalism in your output. For documents that involve complex layouts, it also shows the zoom level and page view mode, allowing for swift adjustments to get the perspective on your document that best suits your current task.

Customizable to fit your workflow, you can right-click on the Status Bar to select which information it should display, tailoring your interface to your specific needs and preferences. The Status Bar is your silent partner in the writing process, keeping you informed and in control as you navigate through the nuances of document creation with Microsoft Word 2024.

2.4. Starting and Configuring the Word Program – Setting Preferences

Embarking on your Microsoft Word 2024 journey begins with starting up the program—where a world of personalization awaits. Tailoring Word to your preferences is pivotal in streamlining your workflow and enhancing productivity. Upon launching, Word greets you with a Start Screen that facilitates immediate access to recent documents or the creation of new ones. This screen can be customized or bypassed, depending on how quickly you want to jump into action.

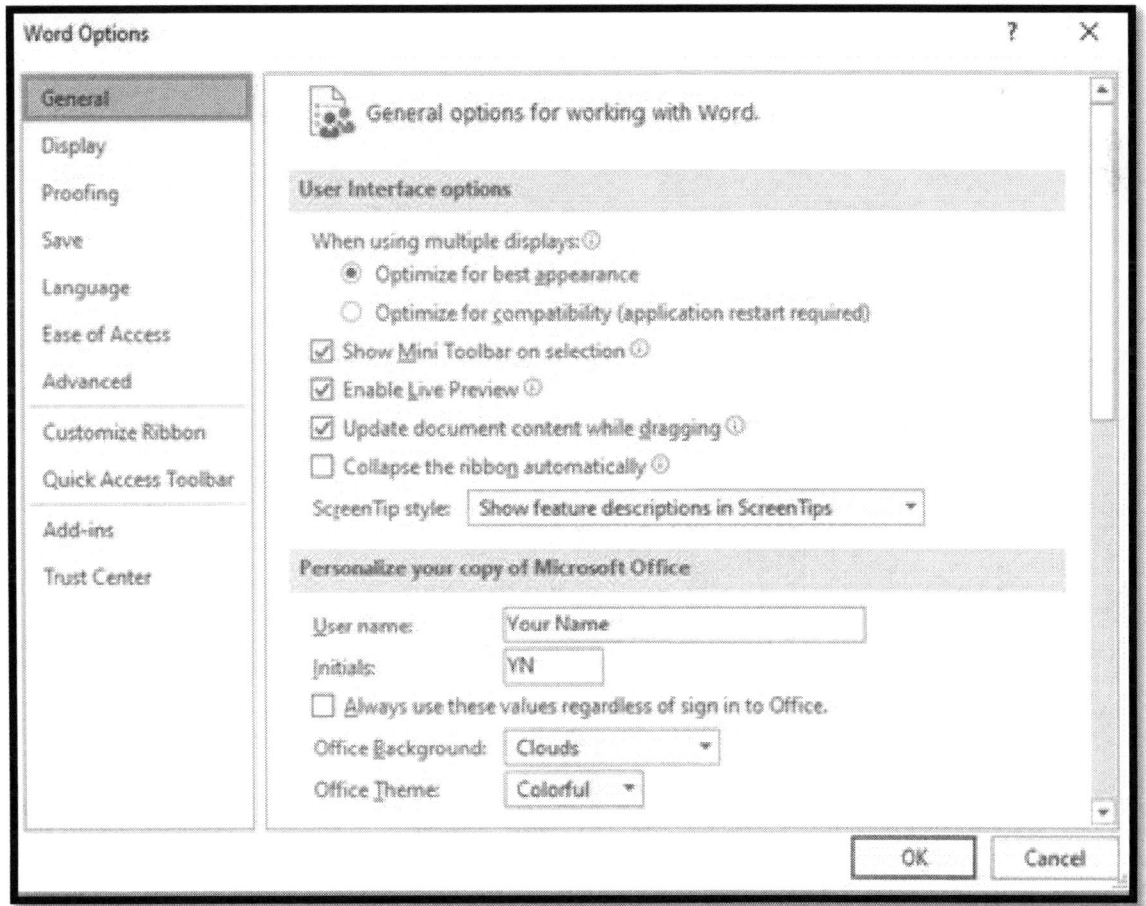

Diving deeper into customization, the 'Options' menu, accessible from the 'File' tab, is your command center for setting preferences. Here, you can configure Word to your writing and design habits. Adjust the default font and size to ensure that every new document aligns with your preferred style. Configure AutoSave intervals to safeguard your work, and define the default document format to match your needs—be it .docx, .pdf, or any other format that Word supports.

Moreover, Word 2024 allows you to set up your proofing options—fine-tuning spell check and grammar recommendations to match your language proficiency or stylistic choices. You can also adjust the Quick Access Toolbar, placing your most used commands within easy reach, optimizing your efficiency.

With these configurations, Word becomes not just a tool, but an extension of your method and style—a program that starts working for you the moment you click into its welcoming interface.

2.5. Working Effectively on the Word Start Screen – Pinning and Recent Files

The Word Start Screen in Microsoft Word 2024 serves as your springboard into document creation and management, offering rapid access to a suite of frequently needed features. Mastering its utility begins with understanding how to navigate recent files and pin those of highest priority.

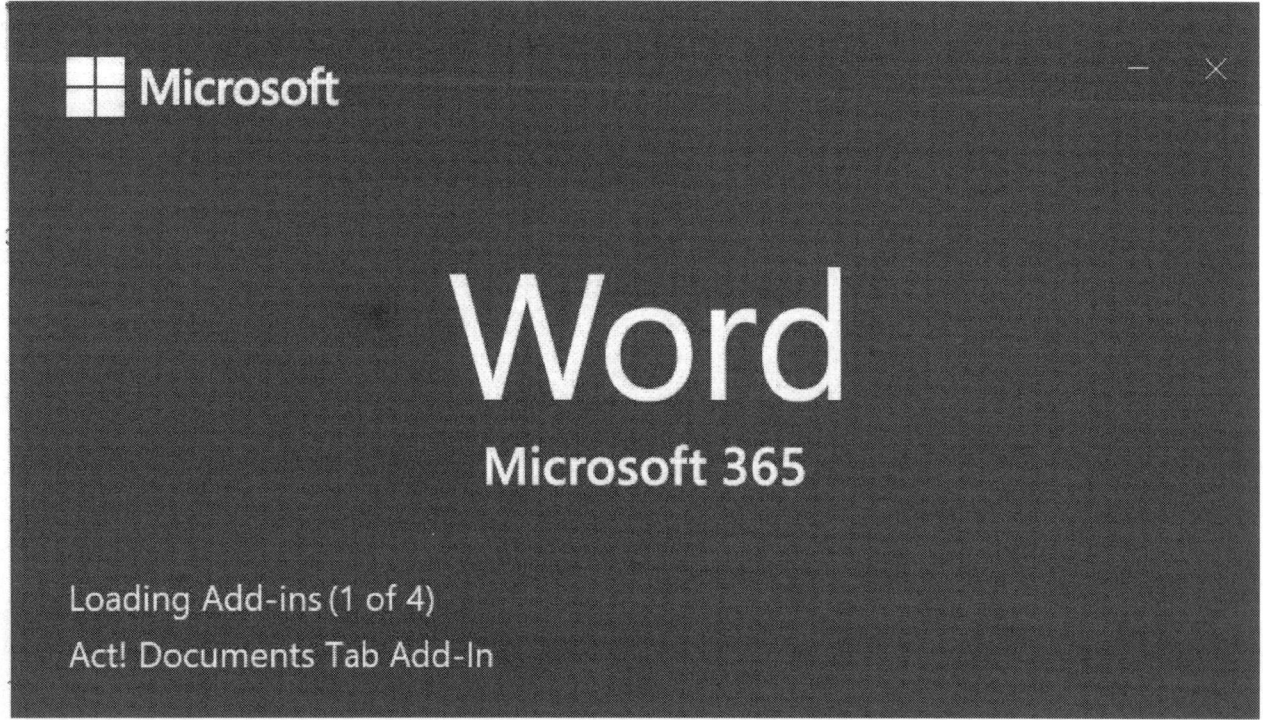

As you open Word, the Start Screen displays a sidebar of recent documents, automatically updated as you work on new files. This history is not just a list but a strategic tool—hover over a document title to see a quick preview and date of last edit, which can be crucial when tracking ongoing projects.

For documents that demand regular attention, the pinning function is a game-changer. By pinning a file, you anchor it to the top of your recent files list, ensuring immediate access regardless of subsequent activities. This is especially beneficial for those working on long-term projects or frequently used templates, streamlining your workflow and saving precious time otherwise spent in search.

The Start Screen also offers the ability to pin folders for quick directory access, further tailoring your user experience. By leveraging these features, you transform the Start Screen from a mere transit point into a customized hub that aligns with your unique document management needs, setting the stage for a more efficient and organized approach to word processing with Microsoft Word 2024.

2.6. Opening, Closing, and Managing Word Documents

Efficiently handling documents is at the core of Microsoft Word 2024's capabilities, ensuring users can smoothly open, close, and manage their work with confidence. When it comes to opening documents, Word provides several straightforward options. You can quickly open recent files from the Start Screen, or use the 'Open' dialogue box to navigate to specific locations on your computer or cloud storage. Word 2024 supports opening multiple documents simultaneously, allowing for easy toggling between files, which is particularly handy for reference or comparison tasks.

Closing documents in Word is just as intuitive. Whether you're done for the day or simply want to clear your workspace, closing a file can be done with a simple click on the 'Close' icon or by using the familiar 'Ctrl + W' shortcut. Word prompts you to save any unsaved changes, so you won't have to worry about losing your latest edits.

Managing documents also encompasses saving them in various formats, using 'Save As' to create copies or templates, and accessing document properties to update metadata. Word 2024's enhanced document management system also includes features for recovering unsaved documents, ensuring that accidental closures or system crashes don't lead to lost work. Together, these tools create a user experience that's both reassuring and conducive to a productive document-handling process.

2.7. Editing Text – Basic Techniques for Styling and Modification

Mastering the art of text editing is essential to harness the full potential of Microsoft Word 2024. Basic text styling and modification are foundational skills that allow you to bring clarity and emphasis to your documents. Starting with the basics, selecting text is as simple as a click and drag with the mouse or a shift with arrow keys. Once text is selected, a wealth of styling options becomes available.

Word 2024 offers a versatile array of fonts and sizes to suit any document need, from professional reports to creative projects. By using the Home tab, you can change font styles, adjust size, and apply bold, italic, or underline options to convey emphasis. For more nuanced styling, the Font dialogue box lets you explore advanced attributes like character spacing, text effects, and typographic details.

Text color and highlight options further expand your ability to make important information stand out. To adjust paragraph alignment, simply choose from left, center, right, or justified alignment buttons, ensuring your text is perfectly positioned for readability and aesthetics.

Editing isn't just about appearance. With Word 2024, you can quickly transform case with the Change Case feature, create bulleted or numbered lists for better organization, and use the Format Painter to replicate formatting across different text sections effortlessly. These basic techniques lay the groundwork for professional, well-styled documents that stand out in any context.

2.8. Saving and Quitting – Preserving Your Work

In Microsoft Word 2024, saving and quitting are more than mere bookends to your document creation process; they are critical steps that ensure the safety and integrity of your work. Saving your document can be a seamless habit with the autosave feature, which quietly preserves your progress at regular intervals. However, for more control, you can manually save your document by clicking the floppy disk icon, pressing 'Ctrl + S', or navigating to 'File' and selecting 'Save' or 'Save As'. The 'Save As' function is particularly useful when you need to create different versions of a document or save your work in various formats like .docx, .pdf, or .odt for broader compatibility.

Quitting Word is just as straightforward but is safeguarded by fail-safes that protect against accidental data loss. When you choose to close Word or press 'Alt + F4', the program will prompt you to save any unsaved changes. It's always a good practice to double-check that your work is saved before quitting, especially when working on lengthy or critical documents.

For added peace of mind, Word 2024 includes features to recover unsaved documents in the event of a sudden shutdown or crash. This means that even if you forget to save before quitting, Word's recovery options can be a safety net to fall back on, reducing the risk of losing valuable work. With these saving and quitting protocols in place, Word 2024 helps ensure that your efforts are preserved for future sessions.

Chapter 3. Mastering Document Creation

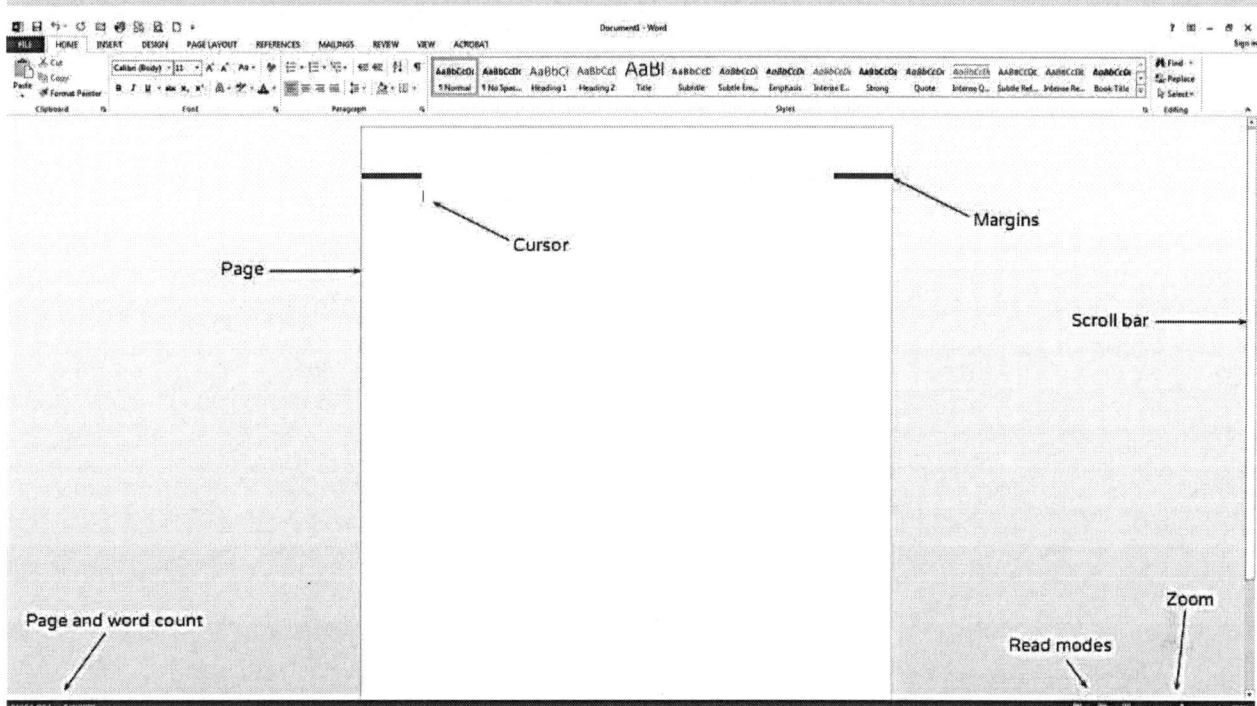

If there are no other gadgets that work with the computer, it will be useless. These diverse gadgets can be used to interface with the computer and do various tasks. This chapter will go over the two main typing input devices as well as everything about typing in Microsoft Word. The image above depicts how the typing screen appears.

Input Devices Set Up

You can enter information into a computer with a device called an input device. The two most important input device is the Keyboard and the Mouse. These two input devices are very important for you to be able to communicate with your computer.

1. The PC Keyboard

A computer keyboard is a piece of hardware that lets you type in data (text, number, punctuations, etc) and commands to a computer. In most cases, your keyboard is the best way to get information into your computer. You can type a letter, number, symbols, punctuation Mark's, etc and you do this by pressing the keys on your keyboard.

How the keys are put together

The keys on your keyboard can be broken down into different groups based on how they work:

- **Using (alphanumeric) keys to type.** These keys have the same letter, number, punctuation, and symbol keys that you would find on a typewriter.

- **The function keys.** The function keys are used to do certain things. They're called F1, F2, F3, and so on, until F12. These keys can do different things in different programs.

- **The navigation keys**. These keys are used to move around and alter text in documents and web pages. There is an arrow next to each of these buttons. The Home and End keys are also present.

- **The numeric keypad**. It makes it easy and fast to enter numbers. All the keys are in a block like on an old calculator or adding machine.

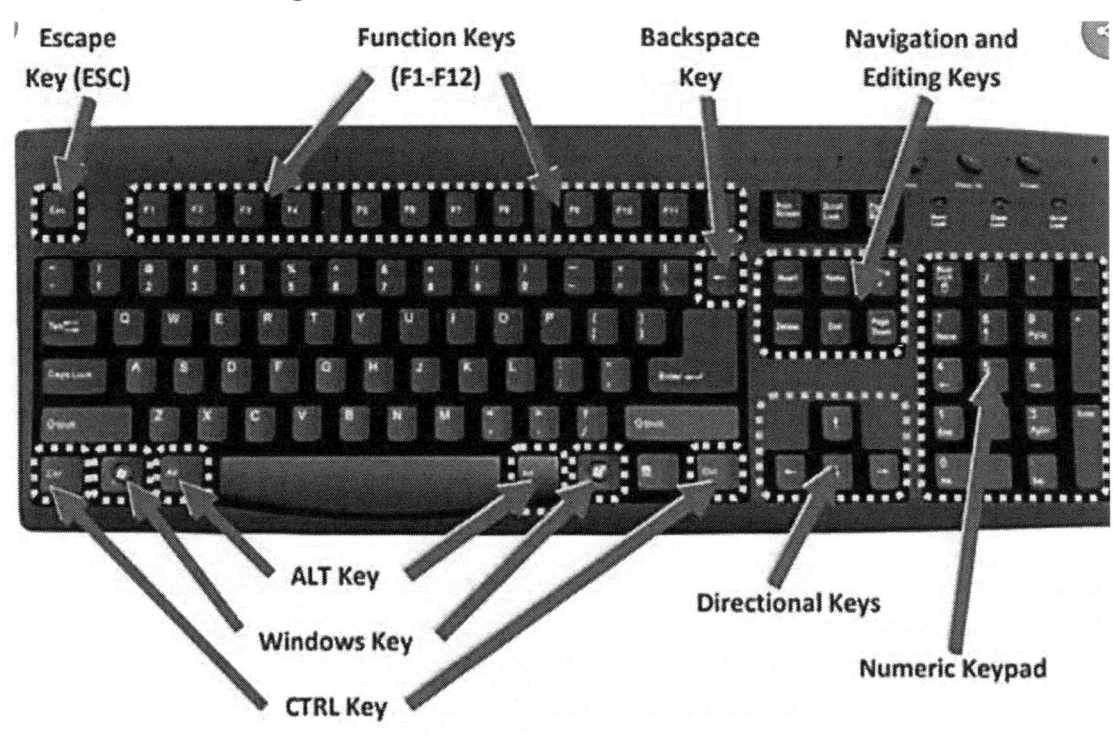

Some major keys in the keyboard are the Shift key, Caps lock, Tab, Enter key, Spacebar, Backspace, Alt key, Arrow Keys.

Note:

- There is a Desktop Keyboard and the Laptop Keyboard.

- Most laptop keyboards don't have a numeric keypad.

- The cursor keys are close together around the typewriter keys in weird and creative ways.

- The function keys may be accessed by pressing certain keys together.

- Each key has two symbols on it, which show that the person has two different personalities.

Putting Words on a Document

When you need to input something in a software, email, or text box, a vertical line blinks. The cursor or insertion point is this line. It indicates where the text you'll write will begin. You can move the cursor by using the mouse to click where you want it to go, or by using the keys. The four arrow keys that go up, down, left, and right can be used to move your cursor in Microsoft Word.

Using the Onscreen Keyboard

When you want to use the On-Screen Keyboard;

- Go to **Start** on your computer

- Then select **Settings**

- Click on **Ease of Access**

- And then click on the Keyboard and turn on the toggle next to Use the On-Screen Keyboard to use the keyboard on the screen

- Immediately, you will see a keyboard that you can use to move around the screen and type text. The keyboard will stay on the screen until you shut it down.

- Open a document in any program where you can write text. Then, with your mouse, click the keys on the onscreen keyboard to type in the text you want.

- To close it, Choose "Close" and then click "OK" on the screen keyboard to get rid of it from your screen.

Note: Here are some things to note about using an on-screen keyboard:

- The onscreen keyboard is nearly identical to a physical keyboard. You can type with your fingers, but you won't be able to do so as rapidly as you would on a real keyboard.

- Some of the special keys (function keys, cursor keys, and so on) are hard to get to. Some of the time, you can get them by switching to a different touchscreen keyboard layout, but most of the time, they're not there at all.

- Using the Ctrl key on the onscreen keyboard requires two steps: first, tap the Ctrl key, and then tap another key.

- Some of the Ctrl-key combinations in Word can't be made by using the on-screen keyboard.

2. The Mouse

The mouse is yet another input device that can be used to type or enter commands into Microsoft Word. You can move the cursor or pointer on a computer screen by dragging it across a flat surface, such as your desk or table, with a mouse. The name "mouse" came to be known as "mouse" because it resembles a little, corded, oval-shaped instrument. Some mice contain built-in functions, such as extra buttons that may be programmed and utilized for various purposes.

Early mouse devices were connected to computers by a cable or cord and had a roller ball built-in as a movement sensor on the bottom of the device. While modern mouse devices are now optical technology, this signifies that a visible or invisible light beam is used to move the cursor. Many models have wireless connectivity through radio frequency (RF) and Bluetooth, among other technologies.

The three main types of the mouse are:

- **Mechanical:** The mouse has a trackball under it and mechanical sensors that make it easy to move in all directions.

- **Optomechanical**: The same as mechanical, but optical sensors instead of mechanical ones are used to detect the movement of the trackball.

- **Optical:** The most expensive. It has no moving parts, uses a laser to detect movement, and reacts faster than previous varieties.

Understanding How The Mouse Pointer Works

A mouse pointer, also called a cursor, is a visible item that shows up on a computer screen. Computer users can move the mouse pointer around the screen by moving the mouse, which moves the mouse pointer. You can move around the document and select text with it too.

The mouse pointer on a computer is typically in the shape of an arrow or a hand. The arrow usually points to the top of the screen and tilts slightly to the left. Arrows represent where the mouse is on the screen, and a line-like pointer shows where text can be inserted in graphical user interfaces. Instead of arrows or hands, text-based interfaces can utilize a rectangle to show where items are.

Cursors often change how they look on a screen because of how they are being used and manipulated on the screen.

- If you want to edit any text, the mouse pointer turns into an I-beam.

- In some documents, users might see hand cursors.

- Mouse pointer 11 o'clock is used to choose items.

- When you want to select lines of text, you use the mouse pointer at 1 o'clock to do it.

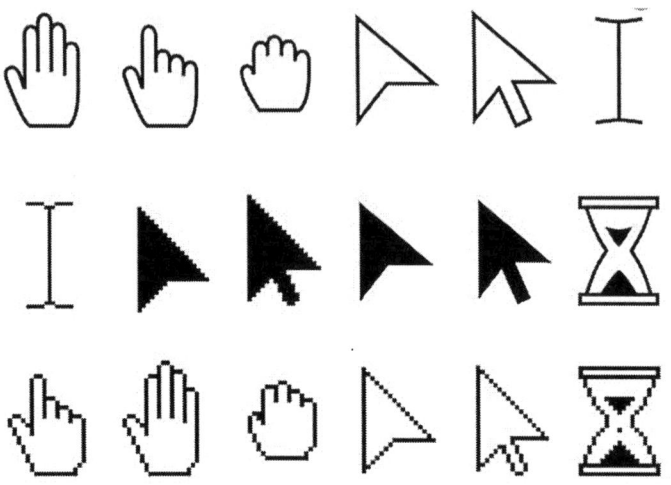

- In some document types, users might be able to press a mouse button and see that the pointer responds by "grabbing" the document page or an object in it.

- When the user is working with graphical editing software, the cursor might change to match the function that he or she is using.

Note: The mouse pointer changes when the click-and-type capability is enabled. Below the I-beam mouse pointer, tiny lines appear to the left and right of the mouse cursor. When you point your mouse at a word tool, you'll see a pop-up information bubble appear. The text in the bubble may provide some insight on how to utilize the command.

Also, in addition, As a person moves the mouse, the mouse pointer will move around the screen in the same way. When the mouse pointer is over a place where text can be typed, the pointer can blink as it thinks about typing. If a user wants to stop the cursor from blinking, he might be able to change the pointer's settings, such as how visible it is and how quickly it blinks. This will depend on the interface.

Keyboard "Do's and Don'ts."

Knowing how to type on a keyboard is essential since it will allow you to learn a few aspects about typing that are specific to word processing. Although learning to type is not required, it is recommended that you do so to avoid unnecessary stress.

i. Following the Insertion Pointer

The text you write in Word shows up where the insertion pointer is. As soon as you move the pointer, it looks like a moving vertical bar: When you move the insertion pointer, a character comes up in front of it one by one. It moves to the right after a character is added, making room for more text.

Note: The Insertion Point can be moved to a new place and the key moves the insertion point to wherever you want it to be.

ii. Pressing the Space Bar

The space bar is used to type blank lines in your text. The space bar is a key on a keyboard that looks like a long horizontal bar. It's in the bottom row, and it's significantly bigger than the rest of the keyboard's keys. You can use it to swiftly enter a space between words while typing.

When typing, the most important thing to remember about the space bar is that you only need to press it once. There is only one space in between words and after punctuation. That's everything!

Note: Any time you think you need two or more spaces in a document, use a tab instead. Tabs are the best way to indent text and to line up text in columns, so they are good for both.

iii. BackSpace and Delete Key

When you make a mistake while typing, you push the backspace key on your keyboard. It deletes a character by moving the insertion pointer back one character. The Delete key also deletes text, but only to the right of the insertion pointer, so it doesn't completely erase it.

iv. Pressing The Enter Key

The Return key is another name for it. It's the keyboard key that tells the computer to enter the line of data or instruction that was just typed into the computer. You only use the Enter key in word processing when you've reached the end of a sentence.

Note: If your text reaches too near to the right margin in Word, it will automatically transfer your last words to the following line. You don't have to press Enter at the end of a line because of this word-wrap feature.

During The Time You Type, Things Happen.

As you type your text quickly, with your fingers pounding the keys on the keyboard, you might see a few things on the screen. You may see spots. lines and boxes that may appear. We are going to look at some major stuff that happens when you type

i. Text Prediction

Microsoft Word helps you write faster as you type. As you type, the app anticipates your next words and presents them for you to accept, allowing you to go through your manuscript faster than ever before. Continue typing after accepting the suggested text with the Tab or Right-arrow key on your keyboard. Simply continue typing or press Esc to dismiss the recommendation.

ii. Keep an Eye on the Status Bar.

A status bar is a type of graphical control element that shows a section of information at the bottom of a window. As you type, it shows you how your document is doing. The status bar shows a collection of information that starts at the left end and moves right.

The information that shows up on the status bar can be changed. It talks about how to control what shows up on the status bar and how to hide things.

It can be broken up into sections so that you can group information. Its main job is to show information about the current state of its window, but some status bars have extra features. For example, many web browsers have sections that can be clicked on to show security or privacy information.

Some good things about status bars: They let you see messages and the whole screen at the same time, they let you write while you look at your status data, status data is shown in a way that lets you see other menu options at the same time and they show how things are going at all times.

iii. Notice the Page Breaks.

A page break in your text indicates where the current page ends and the following one begins. After that, you can click anywhere to open a new page. Click the Insert tab at the top of the screen to add a page break. The Page Break button is on the right of the screen in the Pages group; click it to make the page break visible.

Inserting Page Breaks Manually

It's best to put your insertion point where you want the page break to be. To change the layout of your page, click on the Page Layout ribbon. Then click on Breaks and then choose Page. Page break becomes visible.

Note: The Pages group has a button called "Blank Page." If you want to add a blank page at the break, click on that button.

Remove the Page Break

A page break you put in now can be taken out at any time if you change your mind.

To find and remove page breaks quickly, you should first show the formatting marks.

- Click the **Home button.**

- The **Show/Hide button i**s on the right.

- This shows punctuation characters like spaces, paragraph markers, and the most important for this lesson, page and section breaks.

  - Double-click the **page brea**k to pick it up.

  - Press the **delete key.**

  - The page break is gone.

iv. Collapsible Headers

While typing, you may notice a little triangle to the left of some of your document's headings. You can modify the size of all the text in the header section with these triangles. To hide the text, click once; to reveal it, click twice.

The page does not appear to be empty because of the collapsed sections. They do an excellent job at reducing the size of the page to make it easier to read.

vi. Getting Rid of Spots and Clutter in the Text

Seeing dots or spots in your writing does not necessarily indicate that something is wrong. Characters that can't be read are what you're seeing. Spaces, tabs, the Enter key, and other symbols are used in Word to represent items that are normally hidden. When the Show/Hide feature is enabled, these dots and tittles appear. If you need to remove them again, simply click the Show/Hide button.

vi. Understanding the Colors of the Underlines

When Word underlines your text without your permission, it's alerting you to something that's not right with the way things are going. These underlines are not text styles. At times, you might see these:

- **Red zigzag**: This indicate there is a mistake in the word

- **Blue zigzag**: It indicates errors in grammar and word choice

- **Blue single line**: When you write a document, Word adds blue underlined text to show where web page addresses are. You can press Ctrl+click the blue text to go to the web page.

- **Red lines**: You might see red lines in the margin, below text, or even through text. It means that you're using Track Changes in Word.

Chapter 4. Advanced Editing Techniques

Making text is what typing is all about. Going through and revising your words is also a part of the process. Word contains many commands that can cut, slice, stitch, and so on to assist you with text editing. The instructions are a crucial aspect of word processing, and they perform best when dealing with large amounts of text. Writing initially and then editing is a smart strategy.

Therefore, this chapter will cover how to edit text, how to delete lines and sentences, splitting and joining paragraphs, how to use the Redo command to undo what you did, etc will all be discussed in this chapter.

Deleting a Single Character

When you write in Word, you can use the keyboard to both add and remove text. There are a lot of keys that make text but Backspace and Delete are the only keys that can delete text. These keys become more powerful when they are used with other keys, or even the mouse, that help them delete large amounts of text.

- **The Delete key** removes characters to the **right** of the insertion pointer

- **The backspace key** deletes characters to the **left** of the insertion pointer.

Deleting a Word

The Ctrl and Backspace or Delete keys can be used to delete an entire planet. These keyboard shortcuts can be used in two ways. When the insertion pointer is at the beginning or end of a word, they operate best. When the pointer is in the middle of a word, delete commands are utilized. These commands only delete from that middle point to the start or end of the word. The shortcut to delete is illustrated as;

- The word to the leftward of the insertion pointer is deleted when you press **Ctrl+Backspace.**

- The word to the rightward of the insertion pointer is deleted when you press **Ctrl + Delete.**

Note: When you use Ctrl+Backspace to delete a word to the left. The pointer is at the end of what comes before it. When you use Ctrl+Delete to remove a word, the cursor moves to the start of the next word. This is done to make it easier to quickly remove several words in a row.

Deleting More Than a Word

The keyboard and mouse must work together to remove chunks of text that are bigger than a single letter or single word. The first step is to choose a chunk of text and then delete that chunk of text.

Remove a Line of Text

A line of text starts on one side of the page and goes to the other. If you want to remove the line, you can:

- Make sure the mouse pointer is next to a line of text by moving it to the left.
- Then click on the mouse.
- The line of text is chosen and is shown in a different color on the screen.
- Press the delete key to eliminate that line.

Delete a Sentence

A sentence is a group of text that begins with a capital letter and ends with a period, question mark, or exclamation point, depending on what you're trying to communicate. To do this;

- Place the mouse pointer where the sentence you want to delete lies.
- Press then hold down the Ctrl key at the same time as you click the mouse.
- Using Ctrl and a mouse click together, you can choose a sentence of text that you want to delete.
- The Ctrl key can be let go of, and then you can hit delete.

Deleting a Paragraph

A Paragraph is a group of sentences formed when you press the Enter key. If you want to delete a whole paragraph quickly, here's how to do it:

- Click the mouse **three times.** In this case, the triple-click selects the whole paragraph of the text.
- Press the **Delete button.**

Another way to select a paragraph is to click the mouse two times in the left margin, next to the paragraph, to make it select and then click on delete.

Deleting a Page

Page of text is everything on a page from top to bottom. This part of the document isn't one that Word directly addresses with keyboard commands. To get rid of a whole page of text, you'll need some sleight of hand. Take these steps:

- Press the keys **Ctrl+G.**

- The Find and Replace dialogue box comes up, with the Go To tab at the top of the list of tabs.

- On the Go to What list, choose Page and then type the number of the page you want to remove.

- Click the Go To button, then the Close button. And the page shows up.

- Press the **Delete** button.

- All of the text on the page is taken off.

Split and Join Paragraphs

A paragraph as earlier defined is a group of sentences that all say the same thing about a thought, idea, or theme. In Word, a paragraph is a chunk of text that ends when you press the Enter key. In a document, you can change a paragraph by splitting or joining text.

To split a single paragraph in two;

When you need to start a new paragraph, move the cursor to the desired location. That point belongs at the start of a sentence. To begin, press the Enter key. Word splits the text in half during this process. The paragraph above the insertion pointer becomes the current paragraph, while the paragraph below it becomes the next paragraph.

Making A Single Paragraph Out Of Two Separate Ones

To join two paragraphs together and make them one, simply do this; When you place the insertion pointer at the start of the second paragraph or use the keyboard or click the mouse to move the insertion pointer where you want it to be then press the Backspace button.

This implies that you have removed the entered character from the paragraph before this one thus making two paragraphs into one.

Soft and Hard Return

The **Return or Enter key** is pressed at the end of each line when typing on a keyboard. This indicates that you've finished one paragraph and are ready to go on to the next. However. When you set your page margins, Word knows that when you get to the right margin, your text should wrap to the next line automatically.

There may be times, though, when you wish to stop writing a line before it reaches the right margin. In these situations, you have two options for terminating a line. The first way is to type in the end point of the line and then press Enter. As a result, the document has a hard return on it. This action (pressing Enter) indicates that you've reached the end of a paragraph and want to start a new one.

Another approach to end a line is to hit **Shift+Enter,** which will insert a soft return, also known as a line break or newline character, into the document. The end of a paragraph is indicated by hard returns, whereas the end of a line is indicated by **soft returns.**

A hard return displays on your screen as a paragraph mark (a backward P), while a soft return appears as a down-and-left pointing arrow.

The Undo Command

The Undo command can undo anything you do in Word, like changing text, moving blocks, typing, and deleting text. It does this for everything you do in the program. If you want to use the Undo command, you have two ways to do it:

- The shortcut method is to Press **Ctrl+Z.**

- Alternatively, you can click the Undo command button on the Quick Access toolbar to get back to where your previous work is.

Note: In some cases, you can't use the Undo command because there's nothing to undo. For example, you can't go back and undo a file save.

The Redo Command

If you make a mistake and accidentally undo something, use the Redo command to restore things to their previous state. Assume you type some text and then use Undo to erase it. And, you can use the Redo command to go back and type again. It's your choice. You can choose

- The shortcut method is to press **Ctrl+Y.**

- Alternatively, take a look at the **Quick Access toolbar** and click the **Redo button.**

Note: The Undo command does the opposite of what the Redo command does. So, if you write text, Undo removes the text, and Redo puts the text back.

The Repeat Command

To repeat what you did in Word last time, use the Repeat command to do the same thing again. This could be typing new text, formatting it, or doing a lot of other things.

Using the Repeat command, you can keep the same picture. Whenever there is no more to redo, the Redo command turns into the Repeat command.

To do this:

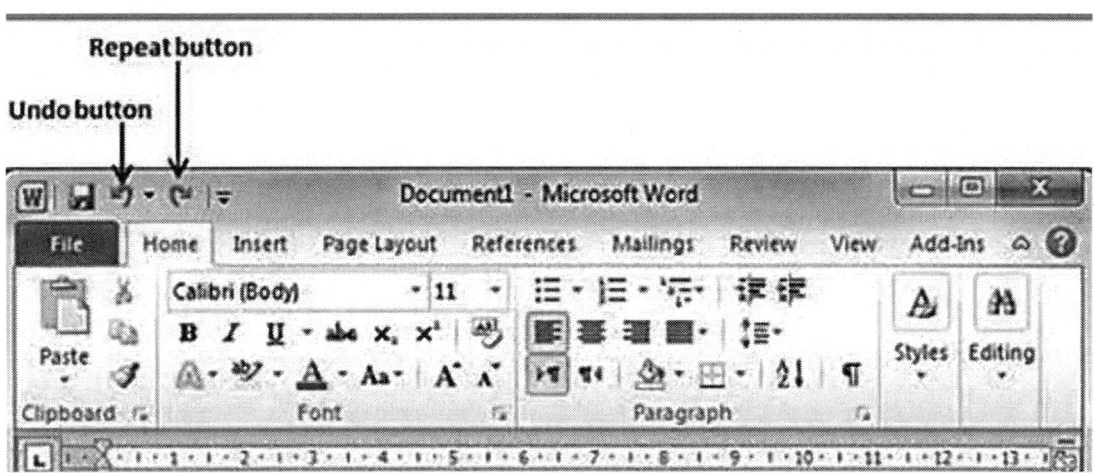

- The shortcut method is to Press **Ctrl+Y**, which is the same keyboard shortcut as to redo something.

Finally, now that you know how to utilize Word's fundamental tools to create a document, this chapter has covered several additional editing tools and easy formatting effects to improve the appearance of a document. Other chapters will go through other editing tools.

Chapter 5. Enhancing Document Presentation

Formatting With Styles And Themes

Styles and **themes** are powerful Word features that you can quickly and easily use to create a professional-looking document. A **style** is a Word predefined combination of all font, and paragraph formatting elements (e.g., font size, font type, color, indent, etc.) applied to a selected text or paragraph. At the same time, a **theme** is a group of formatting choices with a unique set of colors, font, and effects to change the appearance of the entire document.

You can choose from a variety of styles and themes in Word. The steps for applying, modifying, and creating styles and themes are outlined here.

Applying, Modifying, And Creating Styles

To apply a style:

> 1. Select the text or paragraph you want to apply a style.
>
> 2. Go to the **Home** ribbon.
>
> 3. Select the style you want in the **Style** group. You can hover over each style to see the live effect in your document before applying. To see the additional style, click the **More** dropdown arrow.

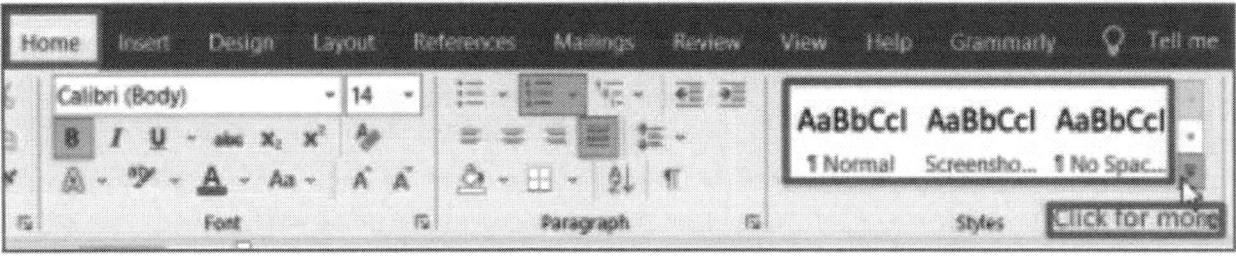

To modify a style:

> 1. Select the style you want to modify.
>
> 2. Right-click and select Modify in the dropdown list.
>
> A **Modify Style** dialog box appears.

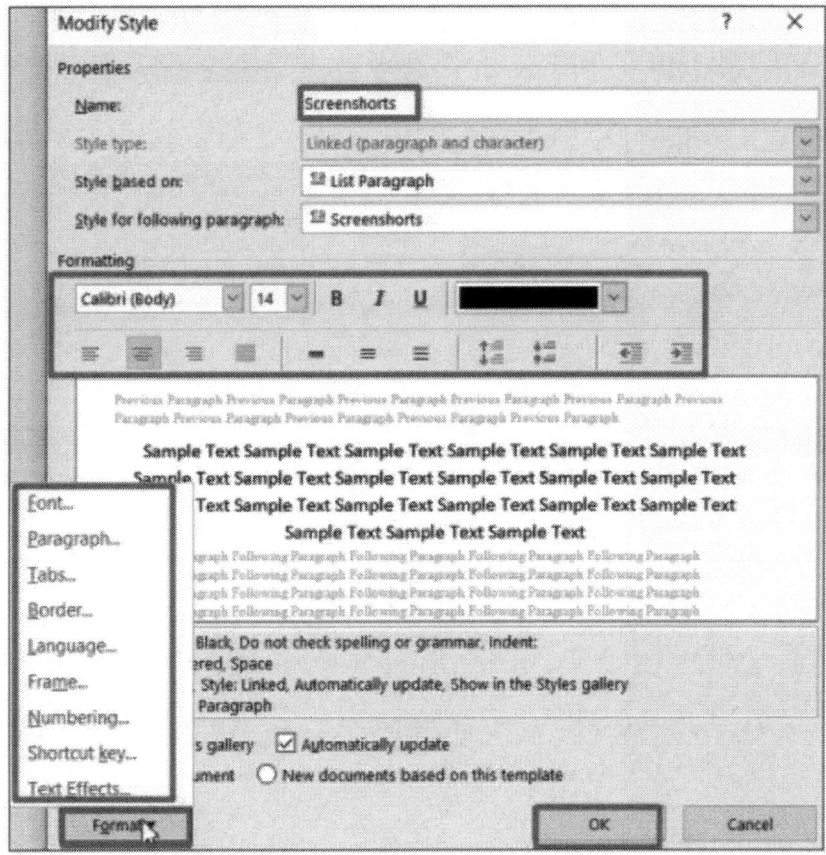

3. Set as desired all the formatting groups. You can as well change the style name.

4. Click on the **Format** button for more formatting options and control.

5. Check the **Automatically update** box to update the styles changes anywhere you have applied them in your document.

6. Press **OK** when you are done.

To create a style:

1. Go to the **Home** ribbon.

2. In the **Style** group, click the **More** dropdown arrow.

3. Select **Create a Style**.

A dialog box appears.

4. Input your desired name.

5. Click the **Modify** button, modify as explained above, and a new style will appear in the style gallery.

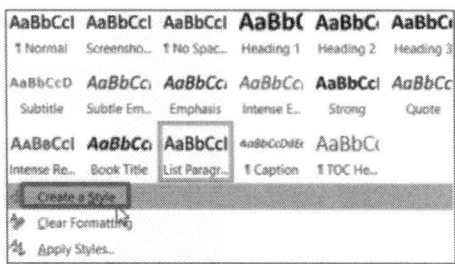

To remove a style from the list, right-click on the style and select **Remove from Style Gallery.**

Creating Your Document With Word Headings

To create your document with Word Headings:

- Go to the **Home** ribbon, under **Style** group.

- Select all your chapters or section headings and click **Heading 1** in the **Style** group.

- Select all the sub-topics or sub-sections and click **Heading 2** in the **Style** group.

- Select all your sub-sub-topics and click **Heading 3** in the **Style** group. Continue to your last headings.

You can customize your headings following the steps in **Section 7.1.1**

Changing, Customizing, And Saving A Theme

A theme is a collection of colors, fonts, and effects that alter the overall appearance of your page. The default Office theme is used whenever you create a document in Word.

To change the theme of your document:

1. Click the **Design** tab.

2. Click the **Themes** command in the **Document Formatting** group.

A drop-down list appears.

3. Hover your cursor over a theme to preview it in your document.

4. Click your desired theme to apply it.

Customizing a theme

You can change any theme element (i.e., color, font, and effect) to create a unique look for your document.

To change themes colors:

1. Go to the **Design** tap.

2. Select **Colors** command.

A drop-down color palette appears.

3. Select the desired color palate or click customize color to combine your colors.

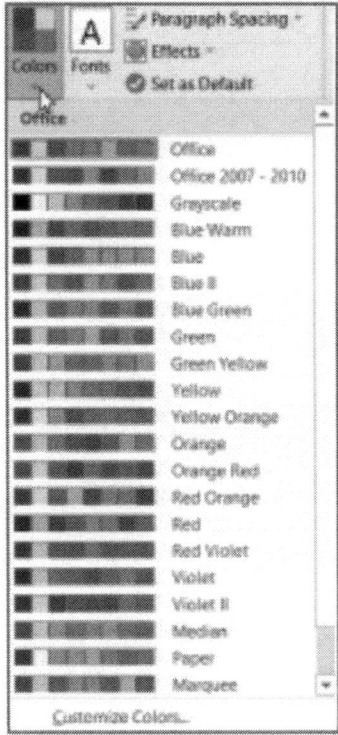

To change a theme font:

1. Go to the **Design** tab.

2. Click the **Font** command.

A drop-down menu of fonts appears.

3. Select your desired theme fonts or

Select **Customize Font** to customize your font. Set your desired font in the dialog box that appears and press **Ok**.

To change a theme effect:

1. Go to the **Design** tab.

2. Click the **Effect** command.

A drop-down list of all the available effects appears.

3. Select the desired effect. You can see the live preview of any effect you hover on.

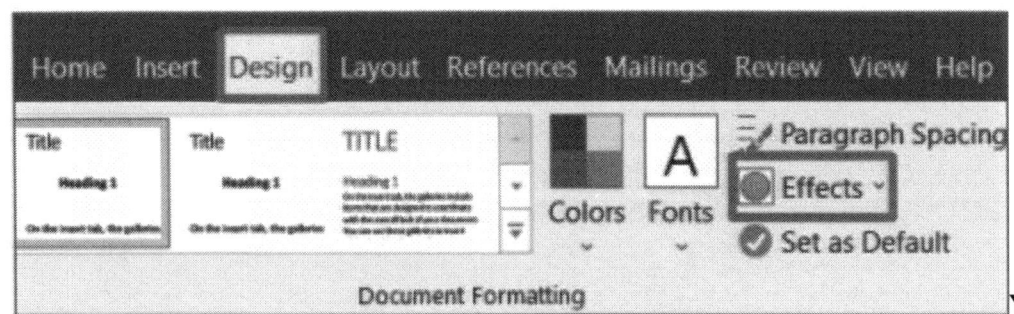You can save your current or customized theme for later use.

To save a theme:

1. Click the **Design** tab.

2. Click the **Themes** command in the **Document Formatting** group.

A drop-down list appears.

3. Select **Save Current Theme**.

4. Input a file name for your theme and press **Save** in the dialog box that appears.

Setting Paper Size, Margins, And Orientation

Margins are the spaces between the edges of your document (top, bottom, left, and right) and your text. They make your work look professional. The default margin in Word is 1 inch for all sides. There are predefined margins, and you can as well customize your margins.

To apply a predefined margin to your document:

1. Go to the **Layout** ribbon.

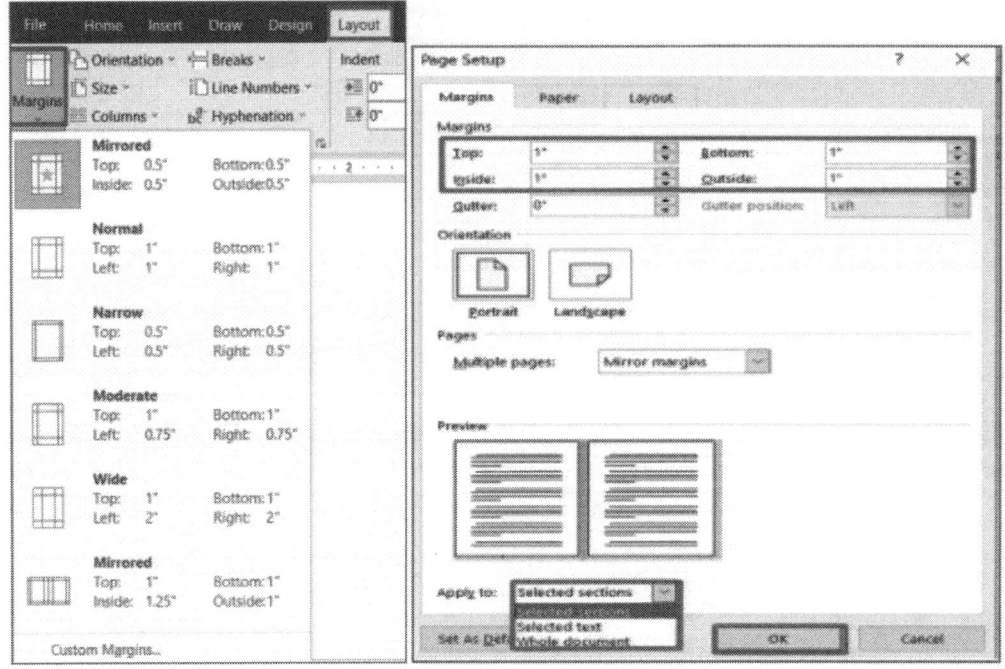

2. Choose **Margins** in the **Page Setup** group.

A drop-down menu appears.

3. Select an option from the list.

To customize your margin:

3. Select **Custom Margins…**

A dialog box appears.

4. Input your values in the textboxes,

5. Select an option in **Apply to:** box.

6. Click **Set As Default** (optional)

7. Press **OK.**

Note: Select the whole document first before applying a predefined margin to a document with different sections because Word applies the predefined margin only to the current section.

PAGE SIZE

To set Page Size:

1. Go to the **Layout** ribbon.

2. Click the **Size** button.

A drop-down menu appears.

3. Select an option from the list.

To customize your page size:

3. Select **More Paper Sizes...**

A dialog box appears.

4. Input your values in the Width and Height text boxes.

5. Select an option in **Apply to:** box.

6. Click **Set As Default** if you wish to set the size as default.

7. Press **OK.**

PAGE ORIENTATION:

To change your page orientation:

1. Go to the **Layout** ribbon.

2. Click the **Orientation** command.

A drop-down menu appears.

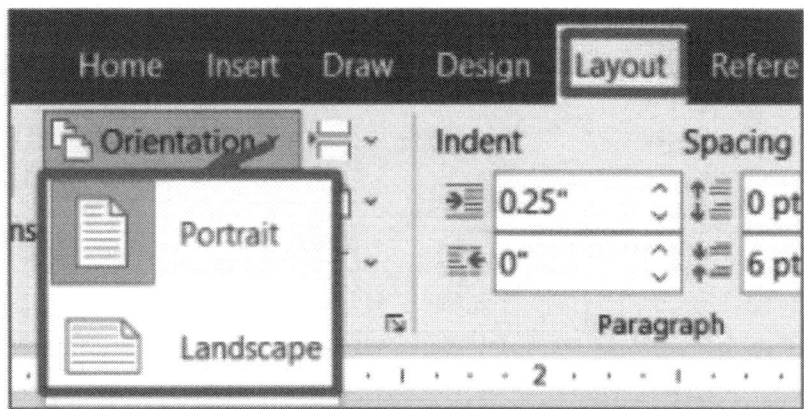

3. Select **Portrait** for a vertical page or **Landscape** for a horizontal page.

Page Breaks And Section Breaks

When working on a document with multiple pages and numerous headings, it might be difficult to format the text so that all chapter heads begin on a new page rather than at the bottom of the previous page. It may also be difficult to add separate headers, footers, footnotes, page numbers, and other formatting elements to some types of documents having several sections, such as an article, report, paper, or book.

Word repeats the headers, footers, and footnotes, as well as the numbering, across the document. Document breaks are required to have a separate one.

There are two types of documents breaks in Word:

- Page breaks
- Section breaks.

Page breaks partition the document's body while section breaks partition not only the document body but also the headings (or chapters), headers, footers, footnotes, page numbers, margins, etc.

Page Breaks are subdivided into:

- **Page break**: This forces all the text behind the insertion point to the next page.

- **Column** break: This forces the text to the right of the insertion point to the next column of the same page when working with a document with multiple columns

- **Text Wrapping break**: It moves any text to the right of the cursor to the following line, and it is instrumental when working with objects.

Section Breaks are subdivided into:

- **Next Page break:** This separates the papers by adding another page with its own formatting. This is helpful for dividing your document into chapters with various headers, footers, page numbers, and so on.

- **Continuous break:** This divides the document into sections that can be independently formatted on the same page without creating a new page. This type of break is usually used to change the number of columns on a page.

- **Even Page break:** This shifts the insertion point and any text at its right to the next even page.

- **Odd Page break**: This shifts the insertion point and any text at its right to the next odd page.

To Insert a Page Break or Section Break:

1. Place your insertion point to where you want the break.

2. Go to the **Layout** ribbon.

3. Select **Breaks** in the **Page Setup** group.

A drop-down list appears with all the types of breaks.

4. Select from the options the type of section break you want.

Inserting Header Or Footer

A header is a piece of text that appears at the top of each page of a document. A footer, on the other hand, is a text that is put to the bottom margin to provide information about the document, such as the title, page number, image, logo, and so on.

To place a Header or Footer to your document:

1. Go to the **Insert** ribbon.

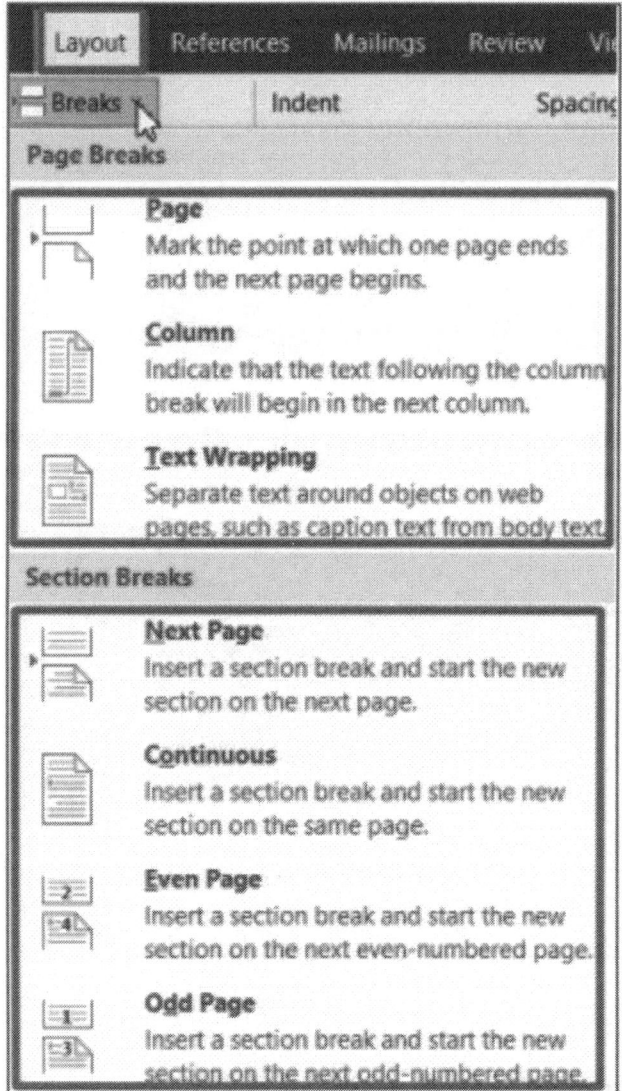

2. Select **Header** or **Footer** command.

A drop-down menu appears with header or footer styles.

3. Click on the desired style.

Word activates the top and bottom margin for your header or footer insertion.

4. Replace the text with your desired text.

5. Click on the **Close Header and Footer** command when you are done.

Alternatively,

1. Double-click in the top or bottom margin to activate the header and footer area.

2. Insert your footer or header.

3. Double click outside the margin area or press the **Esc** key to go back to your document.

You can always use the above method to edit your header or footer. Also available is a contextual **Design** tab you can use to design your header or footer.

To delete your header or footer, just delete the text and close the header and footer.

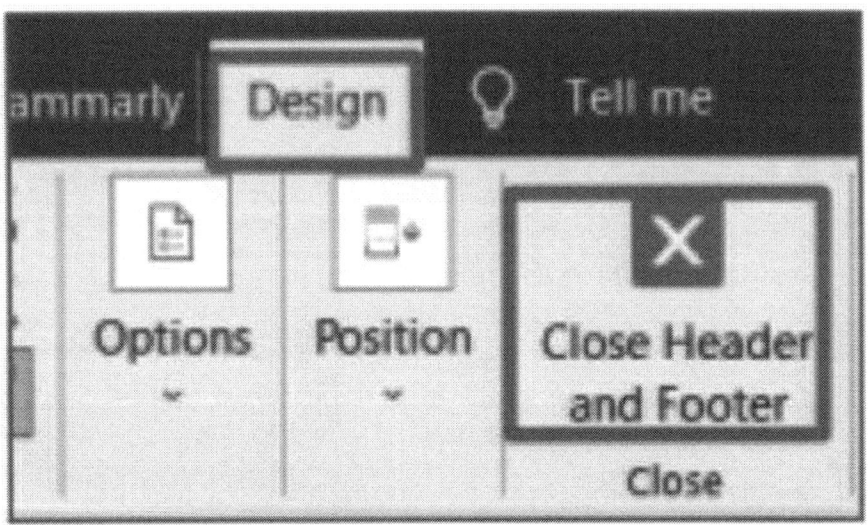

Inserting Different Headers or Footers in Word

To insert a separate Header or Footer for a Separate Section:

1. Insert **Next Page** section breaks to where you want different headers or footers to start.

2. Activate the headers or footers of each section.

In the **Navigation** group of the **Header & Footer** Tools ribbon;

3. Deselect the **Link to Previous** button to disconnect the sections.

4. Add the header or footer for each section or chapter.

5. To put a different header on the first page of the document or a section, Check the **Different First Page** box.

6. To put a right-justified header for some pages and a left-justified header for some pages, check the **Different Odd & Even Pages** box.

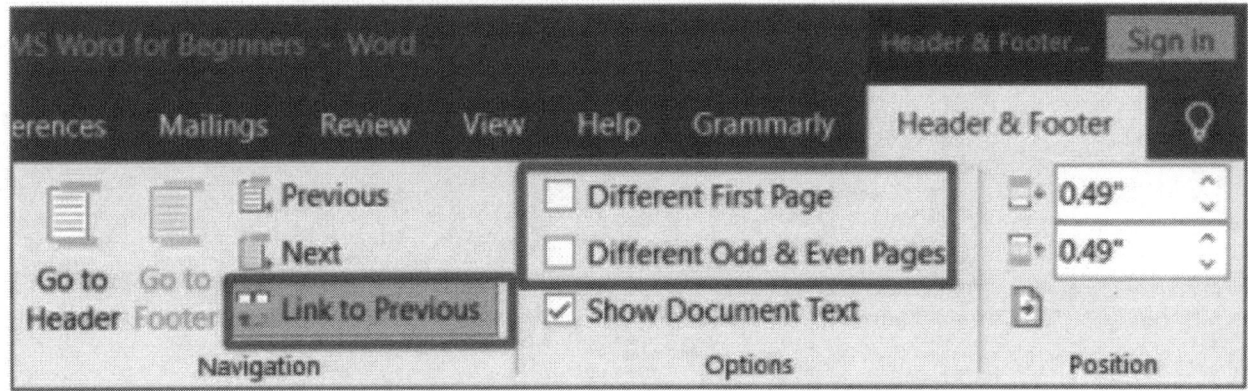

7. Close the header/footer when done with the settings.

Saving Headers Or Footers For Later Use

If you frequently generate documents with the same header or footer, it's a good idea to store the header/footer.

To save your header or footer for later use:

1. Activate and select all the header or footer contents you want to save.

2. Click the **Header** or **Footer** drop-down button as the case may be.

3. Select **Save Selection to Header Gallery** or **Save Selection to Footer Gallery,** depending on whether you select Header or Footer.

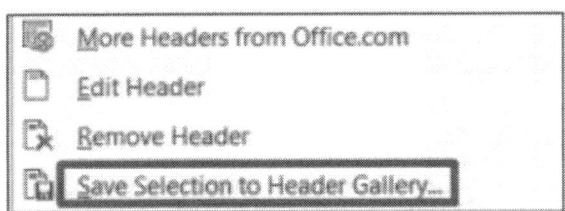

A dialog box appears.

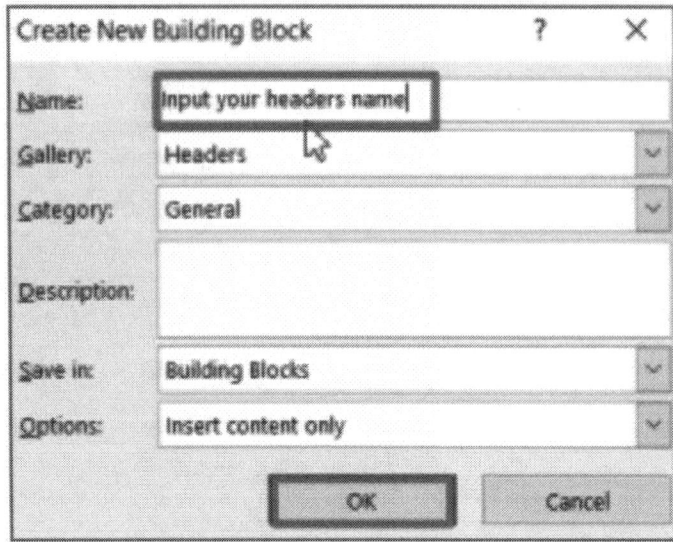

4. Input the name you want to give the header or footer and do any other desired settings.

5. Press **OK,** and your header or footer will be saved.

You can access and apply the header or footer at any time in the drop-down list of the **Header** or **Footer** drop button. You might have to scroll down to see your

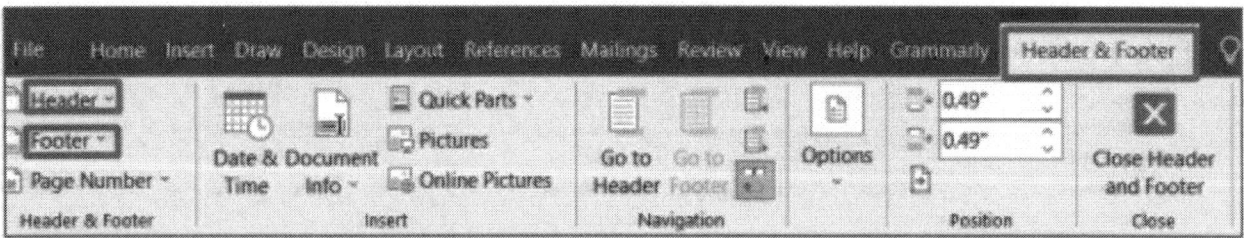

To delete your saved header or footer:

1. right-click on it.

2. Select Organize and Delete.

A dialog box appears highlighting the header or footer.

3. Click the **Delete** button.

4. Press **yes** to confirm the prompt that appears.

5. Press **Close** in the dialog box, and your header or footer will no longer be in the gallery.

Page Numbering

To add page number to your document:

      1. Click the **Insert** tab.

      2. Select **Page Number** button in the **Header & Footer** section.A drop-down menu appears with the list of where you can insert your page number.

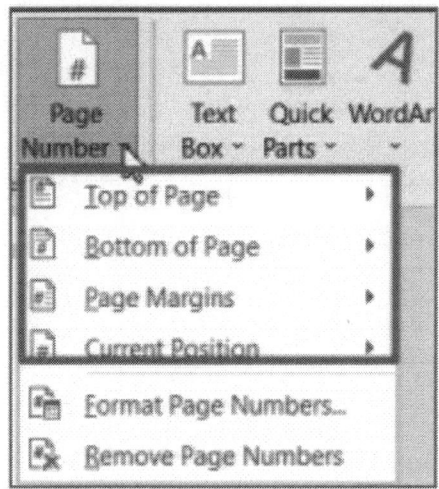

      3. Select an option.

A dialog box with page number styles appears.

      4. Click your desired style.

Word assigns page numbers to all of your document's pages and activates the header and footer areas.

      5. Right-click on the page number or Click the **Page Number** command in the **Headers & Footers** ribbon for settings

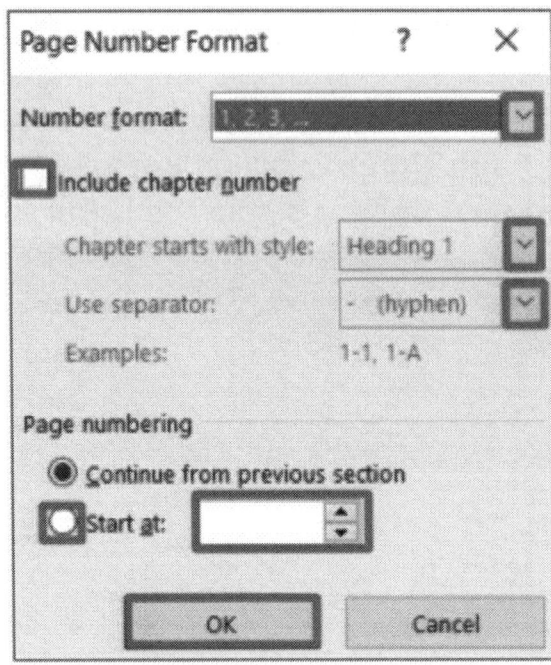

A dialog box appears.

6. Select the drop-down button to select the **Number format** you want.

7. Check the **Include chapter number** box to include chapter numbers, select the **Chapter starts with style** and **Use separator** options (optional).

8. Check the **Start at** button and set the start value if you do not want the numbering to continue from the previous section (applicable for setting different page numbering for different sections).

9. Press **OK**.

10. Double click outside the margin to go back to your document area.

Inserting Different Page Numbers.

To insert different page numbers to your document:

1. Insert page number to the entire document first, following the above steps.

2. Create section breaks to the document where you want different page numbers.

If you have different chapters in your document, it is advisable to create **Next Page** section breaks for each chapter and prefatory sections. (Check **section 7.3** for the steps)

3. Double-click the header or footer of the section you want to change the page number.

4. Locate and Deselect the **Link to Previous** button in the **Navigation** group of the **Header & Footer Tools** ribbon if needs be.

5. Right-click on the page number or Click the Page Number command in the Headers & Footers ribbon to set the page numbers as desired.

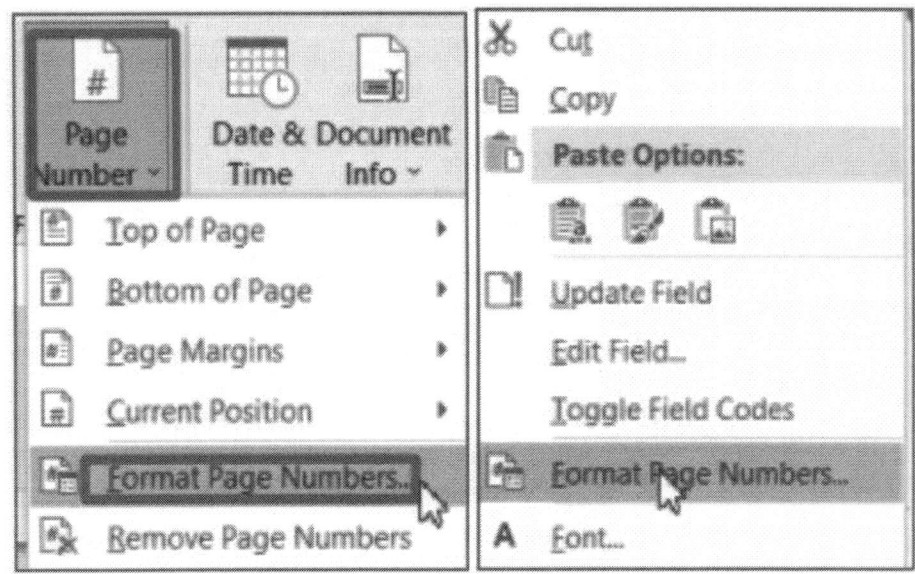

6. Continue **steps 3-5** above for all the sections as desired.

Removing Page Numbers.

To remove Page numbers from the entire document:

1. Go to the **Insert** ribbon.

2. Click **Page Number**.

A drop-down menu appears.

3. Select **Remove Page Number** from the options.

Alternatively,

1. Double-click on the Header or Footer area.

2. Select the page number and press the **Delete** key.

To remove the page number from the first page of the document or a section:

1. Double-click in the margin of the section or document to activate **Headers & Footers** Tools.

2. Check the **Different First Page** box in the Options group.

You can also check the **Different Odd & Even Pages** box to remove page numbers of alternate pages.

Inserting Automatic Table Of Content

Microsoft Word includes a tool that lets you create a table of contents either automatically or manually using simple templates. You must write or prepare your document using the Word built-in headings in the Styles group to automatically insert a table of contents. (Check **section 7.1.2** for how)

To Insert a Table of Contents:

1. Ensure your document headings uses Word built-in headings styles

2. Place your insertion point where you want the table of content to be.

3. Go to the **References** ribbon.

4. Click **Table of Contents**.

A drop-down menu appears.

5. Select an option:

• The first two options automatically insert your table of contents with **all** your available headings.

• The third option inserts the table of contents with placeholder texts and allows you to replace them with your own headings.

- Select **More Tables of Contents from Office.com** for more templates.

- Select the **Custom Table of Contents...** to customize your table. A dialog box appears, edit as desired, and press **OK**.

- If you already have a table of content in your document, you can delete it by selecting **Remove Table of Contents.**

Updating your Table of Contents

Word does not update your table of content automatically if you make changes to your document. You will have to update it manually.

To update your Table of Content:

1. Position your cursor in the table of content.

Table borders appear with buttons at the top-left.

2. Click the **Update Table** button.

A dialog box appears.

3. Click the **Update entire table**.

4. Press **OK**.

Word automatically updates your table.

Alternatively,

1. Right-click on the table of content.

A drop-down menu appears.

2. Select **Update Field.** You can also select **Update Table** in the **Table of Contents** group in the **References** ribbon.

A dialog box appears.

3. Click **Update the entire table**.

4. Click **OK**.

Note: Do not always forget to update your table after making significant changes that affect the headers or page numbers.

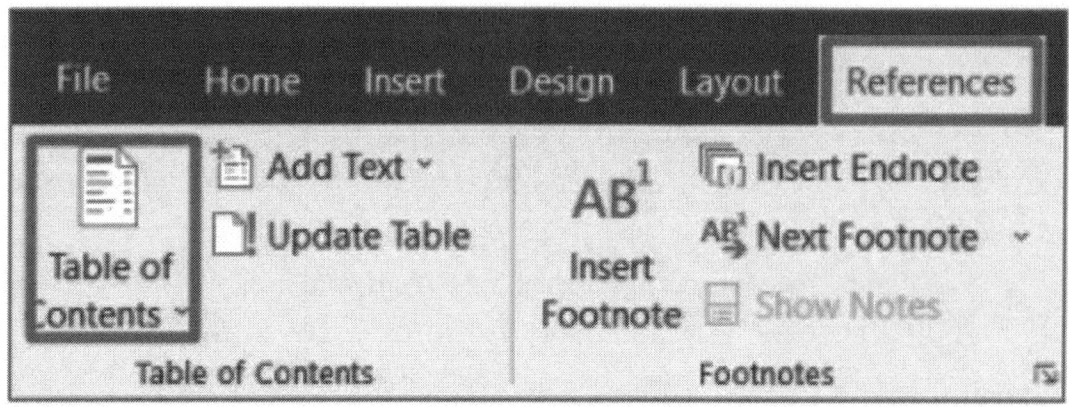

Adding Captions To Figures Or Objects

A caption is a title or brief explanation of a figure or an object mostly placed below a figure or an object to give information about the figure.

To add a caption to an object:

1. Select the object you want to add a caption to.

2. Go to the **References** tab.

3. Click **Insert Caption** in the **Captions** group.

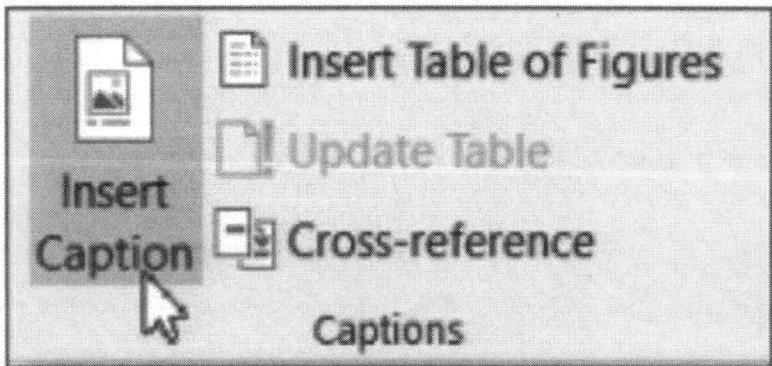

A caption dialog box appears.

4. Select **Figure** in the **Label** dropdown menu or any appropriate options.

5. Type the object description (it can include punctuations) in front of **Figure 1** in the **caption** text field.

6. Click **OK.**

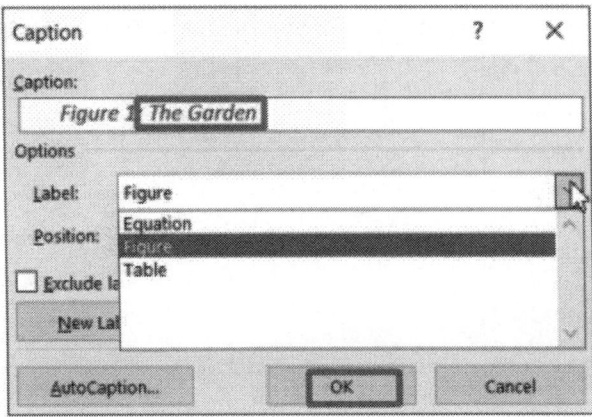

You can **format** your captions in the **Styles** group of the **Home** tab following the steps in **section 7.1**

To Add Chapter Number that updates automatically to your Image Caption.

1. Ensure you format your document headings with the Word **Headings** in the **Style** group. (Check **section 7.1** for more information).

2. Use the Word Multilevel list to number your chapter headings or **Heading 1** as the case may be following the steps below:

- Select any of your Chapters or Heading 1 style.

- Go to the **Home** tab.

- Click the **Multilevel List** icon in the **Paragraph** group.

- Select **Chapter 1 Heading…,** the last option, and all Headings 1 will be numbered automatically.

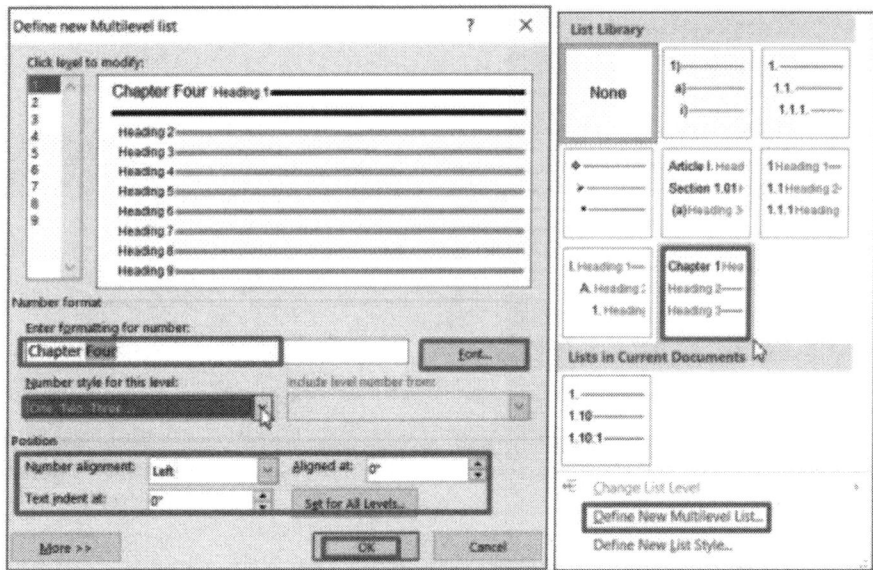

You can format the numbering in **Define new Multilevel** list. You can change the Chapter to a Section, change the numbers to words, change the font, and so on.

3. Select the object you want to add the caption.

4. Go to References >> Captions >> Insert Caption.

5. Select **Numbering** in the **Caption** dialog box.

A **Caption Numbering** dialog box appears.

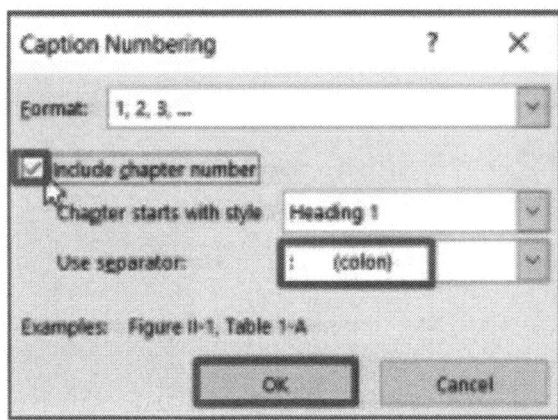

6. Check the **Include chapter number** box, select the desired separator, and press **OK**.

To make your captions sticks to your floating object:

1. Select the Object.

2. Go to the **Layout** tab.

3. Select **Wrap Text** command.

4. Choose any other options aside from the first from the dropdown list as desired. Alternatively, you can click on the Layout button at the top right corner of the object and select an option in the **With Text Wrapping** list.

5. Add a caption to your figure following the above steps.

6. Group the caption and the object (follow the steps in **section 5.11.3**)

To Delete a Caption: Select the caption and press Delete.

Note: Word automatically updates the figure numbers as you insert a new caption. You must update the caption or figure numbers whenever you delete or change the position of any caption.

To update the caption numbers:

1. Select all your document using **Ctrl + A**.

2. Right-click and select **Update Field** in the dialog box that appears **or**

Press **F9** to update the caption numbers.

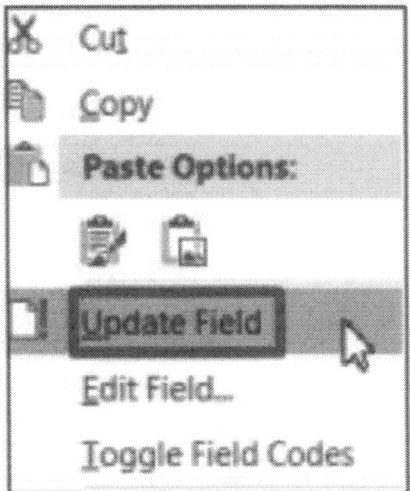

Inserting Automatic Table Of Figures

Word has a command to automatically add a table of figures to your work, just like adding a table of contents.

For you to automatically generate a table of figures, you must have added captions to all the figures used in your document using the Word **Insert Caption** command.

To Insert Table of Figures:

1. Ensure that you use the Word caption feature to add captions to your objects.

2. Place your insertion point where you want the table of figures to be.

3. Click the **References** tab.

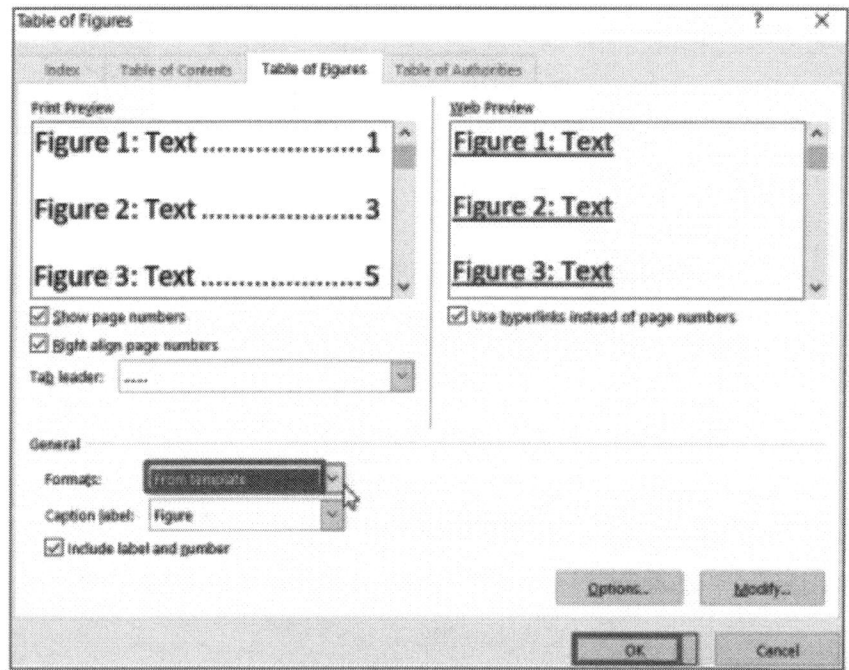

4. Select **Insert Table of Figures** in the **Caption** group. Table of Figures dialog box appears.

Select your desired Format, make other changes, preview, and press **OK**. Your table of figures appears in your document.

Inserting Cover Page

A cover page contains information about the document like the title, author, and other enticing objects or texts.

To insert a cover page:

1. Go to the **Insert** ribbon.

2. Click the **Cover Page** button in the **Pages** group.

A drop-down menu appears.

3. Select the desired templates to customize.

4. Edit, format, and the template to your taste. You can add images, text, and so on.

Working With Citations

Citation is a standard technique in academic writing that informs readers about the sources of quotes or paraphrases used in your text. To save you time and frustration, Word provides a tool that assists you with citations.

To insert Citation into your document:

1. Position your insertion point wherever you want to place your citation.

2. Click the **References** tab.

3. Click (Placeholder1) **Insert Citation** in the **Citations & Bibliography** group.

A drop menu appears.

4. Select **Add a New Source** option.

A dialog box appears.

5. Select the **Type of Source** (e.g., book, journal, article, etc.) using the dropdown arrow.

6. Fill in the source details in the text boxes provided.

7. Check the **Show All Bibliography Fields** for additional information.

8. Input the **Tag name**.

9. Press **OK,** and your citation is inserted.

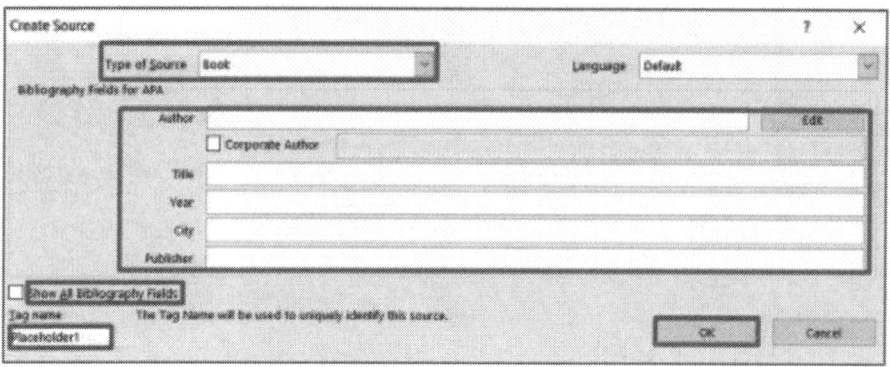

Inserting References, Works Cited, Or Bibliography

A bibliography is an alphabetical list of all sources you consulted for your document, whether or not you cited them. References and works cited are alphabetical lists of all the citations used in your document, whereas a bibliography is an alphabetical list of all sources you consulted for your document, whether or not This list is frequently seen towards the conclusion of a text.

The format style utilized distinguishes references from works cited. Different professional and academic groups use a variety of citation styles. When referencing works in APA (American Psychological Association) format, use references, and when citing works in MLA (Modern Language Association) format, use works cited list.

To insert References, Works Cited List, or Bibliography:

>1. Ensure you use the Word **Citation** command to cite in your document body.

>2. Place your insertion point wherever you want the lists to be.

>3. Click the **References** tab.

>**4.** Click **Bibliography** in the **Citations & Bibliography** group.

>A drop-down menu appears.

>5. Select an option, and it appears in your document.

Note: Any time you edit or add to the citations in your document, you must manually update your references, works cited, or bibliography. This can be done from the list or any of the citations in the document.

To Edit and update your citations:

- Select any of the citations in the document.

- Right-click on the citation or click the drop-down arrow.

- Select **Edit Source** from the menu that appears, edit the **Create source** dialog box, click **Ok,** and click **yes** to the prompt that appears.

- **To update**, click **Update Citations and Bibliography** instead.

or

- Select the references or bibliography.

- Click on the **Update Citations and Bibliography** button at the top left corner of the list border.

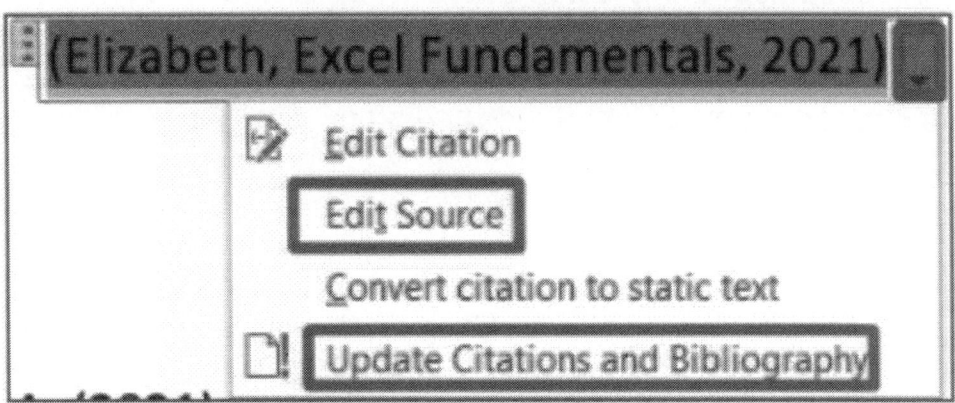

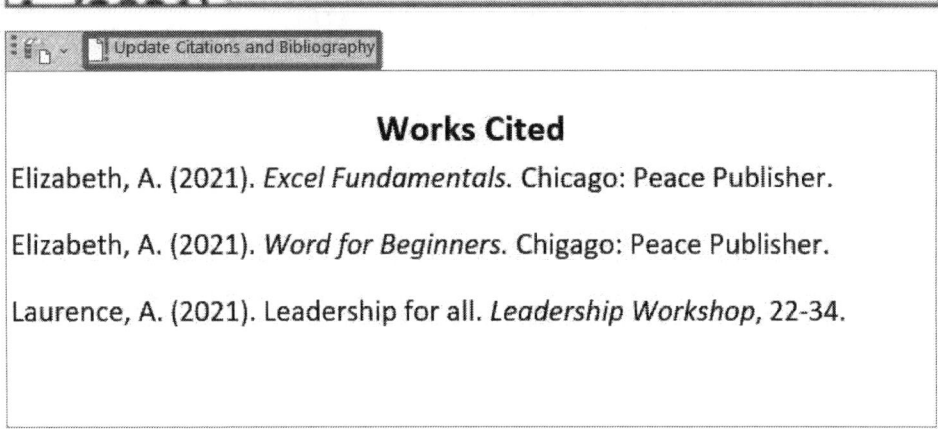

Works Cited

Elizabeth, A. (2021). *Excel Fundamentals*. Chicago: Peace Publisher.

Elizabeth, A. (2021). *Word for Beginners*. Chigago: Peace Publisher.

Laurence, A. (2021). Leadership for all. *Leadership Workshop*, 22-34.

Chapter 6. Organizing Complex Content

We'll learn how to build, insert, and remove borders, rows, and columns in this chapter. We'll also go through how to make a table of contents, a bullet and numbering list, an endnote, and footnotes in Microsoft Word, as well as the visuals.

Borders

A border is like a line coupled into a text, paragraph, or page of a document. This line can be in a different format, either thin or thick, single, double or triple, dashed, or with various art and color

Insert A Page Border In Microsoft Word 2023

Open a new or existing document on your computer. Then, on the Ribbon, select the Design tab. Then, on the page border, click. Scroll down to the borders and shading section. The dialogue box with the borders and shading appears. Select any type in the options section. box, 3D, shadow, and so on Click Apply to, which will enable you to select where you want it to appear on the document, and then click Ok. You can also change the color, style, art, and width of the border.

How To Add Border To A Part Of Text

Select the text you want to apply the border to. Click on the **page border** on the design tab and the dialogue box, click on any type and click Ok. The border will be added to that selected text in the document. Note you can also edit your border with the elements shown in the figure

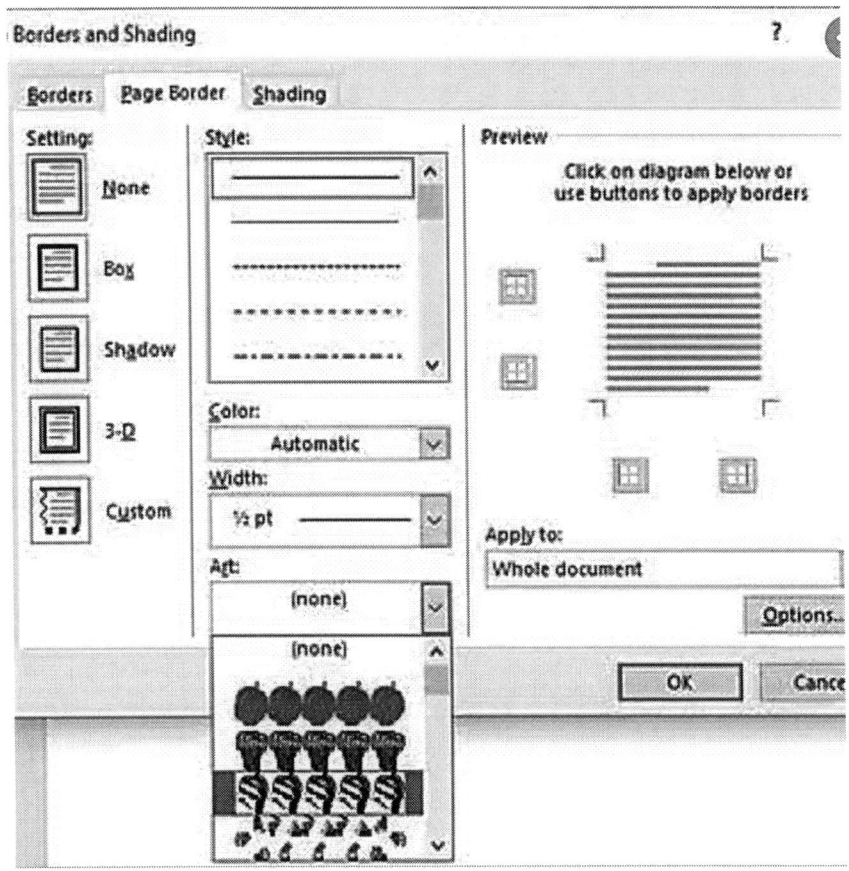

How To Add Border To A Paragraph

Select the paragraph. Click on the border on the design tab and click OK to apply a border to a paragraph.

To Remove A Border

Click on the None option on the dialogue box that pops up when you click on the page border button on the Design tab.

The Table On Microsoft Word 2023

How To Insert A Table

To begin, open a document on your computer. Place your cursor where you want the table to appear in the document. Select the table from the table group from the Insert tab. Move your cursor across and down to select the number of cells in your table that will be grouped as rows and columns. The selected cells will turn orange then click Insert table.

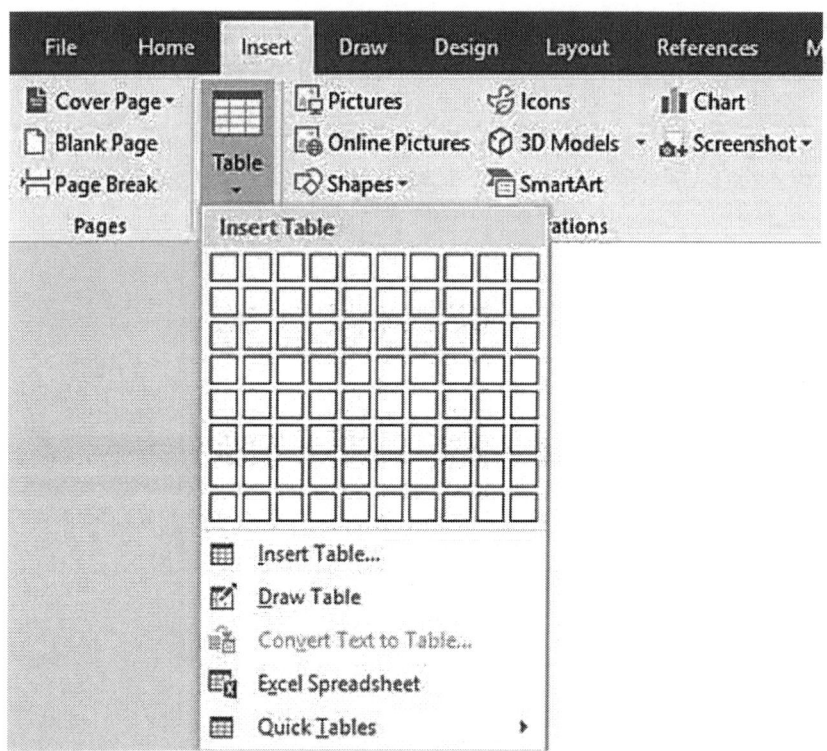

Quick Table

Quick tables are tables that you can change to suit your needs. To begin, place your cursor where you wish the table to be inserted. On the Ribbon, select the Insert tab. As indicated in the figure, select table from the table group, then fast table from the drop-down menu. From the gallery, select the table you desire. Then type over or delete the table example text to fill in your material.

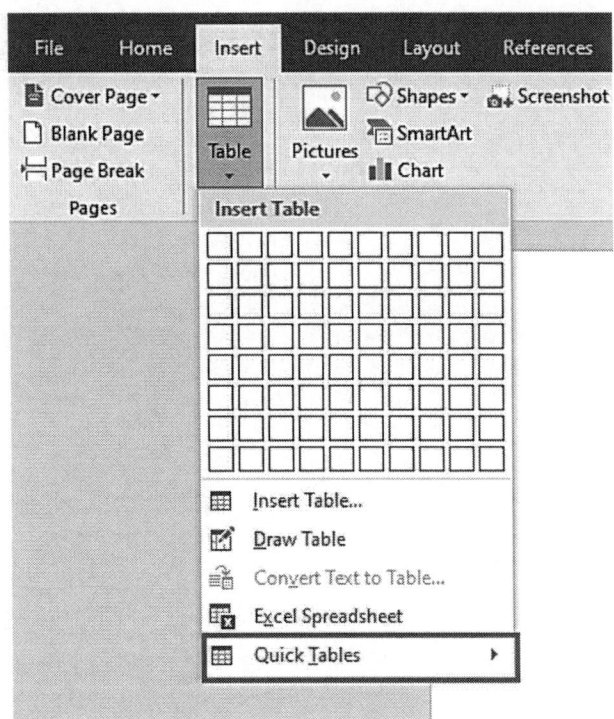

How Do I Enter Text Into A Table

To do this, place your cursor into a cell and type as you normally would enter a text into a table.

Table Styles

Click on the Design tab and then on Table Style, click on the drop-down button circled in the figure below, and different table styles show up then you can select any one of them.

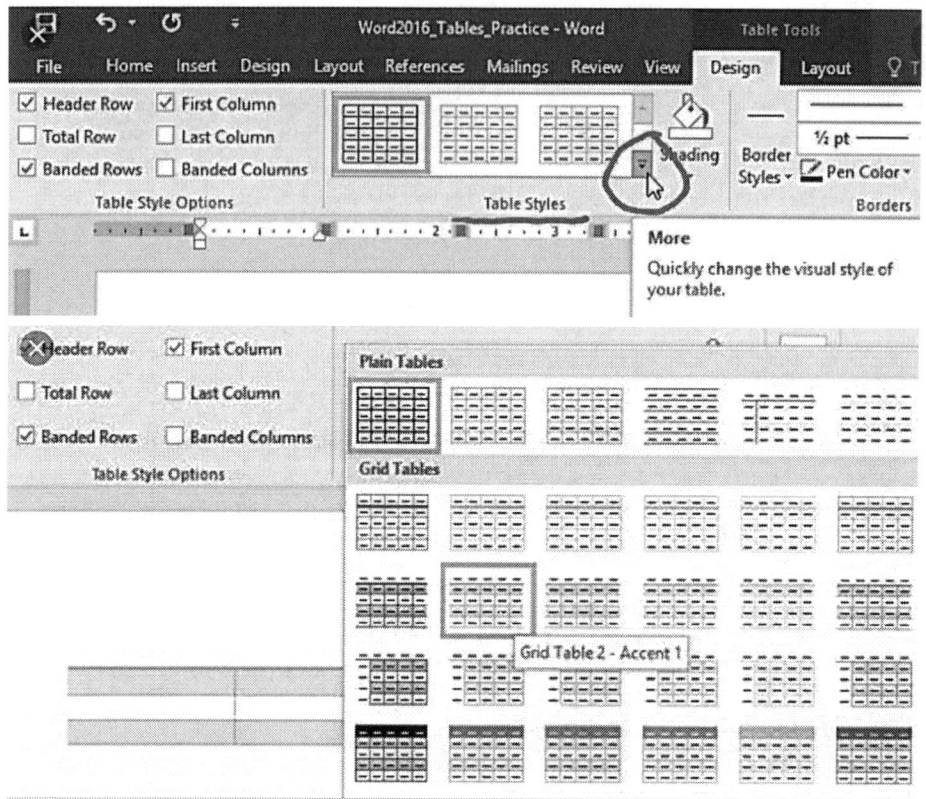

Note: You can use the shading menu to add a custom menu to individual rows and columns.

- **Header Row:** Only the header row is colored, the first row is highlighted
- **Banded Rows:** Alternate rows are highlighted
- **Total Row**: All rows are highlighted
- **First Column:** The first column is highlighted
- **Last Columns:** last columns are highlighted
- **Banded Column:** Alternate Column are highlighted

To Create Your Table Styles

Click on create new table style on the table style group and do lots of formatting on the dialogue box. Click okay when you're done.

Insert Rows And Column

Place your cursor beneath any row to add another row once you've created a table. Select the plus sign. To add a column, go to the layout tab and select Insert left, insert above, insert right, or insert bottom from the drop-down menu.

Simply set your cursor where you want to add the column and click Insert column, then choose any location where you want the column to be placed, and your document will be modified.

Cut/Copy/Paste/Delete Rows And Columns

Click on the row and column on the Layout tab, you will see delete. Click on it to delete the column or just right-click with your mouse. It displays different options to cut, copy, paste or delete rows and column

Alternatively, to delete a table, select the table selector which is a + plus. It will select the entire table. Note that you may have to use the pointer over the table to reveal all the table selectors. Then right-click the table and select the delete table from the shortcut menu,

Resize Rows, Column, And Tables

Place your cursor in any column, then select the layout tab and cell size group. There is a height choice; click it to expand it, and the column's height will increase, as will the weight.

To make each column the same height, click distribute rows, and all rows will be the same height. To get an equal column, do the same thing with the column. Click on distribute column.

Click the resizing lever in the bottom right corner of the table to resize the entire table. To reveal the handle, you may need to slide your pointer over the table. Then, using the + sign on the table's bottom side, move the table to the desired size.

Split And Merge Cells

Select all the cells, click on the layout tab and click on merge cells while on split cell place your cursor on the cell, click on split cell, a dialogue box shows up to type in how many rows and columns you want, type in the number and click OK. That cell will be split into the number of rows and columns you typed in.

To split an entire table, keep your cursor anywhere you want to split the table. Click on the split table and it will be split.

How To Convert Text To Table

Select your text first. Click the drop-down arrow on the table groupings under the Insert tab. To convert text to a table, scroll down. Select a text separation option from the dialogue box. This is how Word determines what should go into each column. Then press OK.

Placing A Column Break

You can break a column in Word just like you can break a page. Only multicolumn pages can have this column break. It is beneficial for the column's text to come to a halt somewhere on the page and then resume at the top of the next column.

To do this: Click to place the insertion pointer in your document which will be the start of the next column and click the **Layout** tab. Thereafter, click on the **break** button located on the **page setup group**. A menu appears to click on the column. The text immediately moves to the top of the next column.

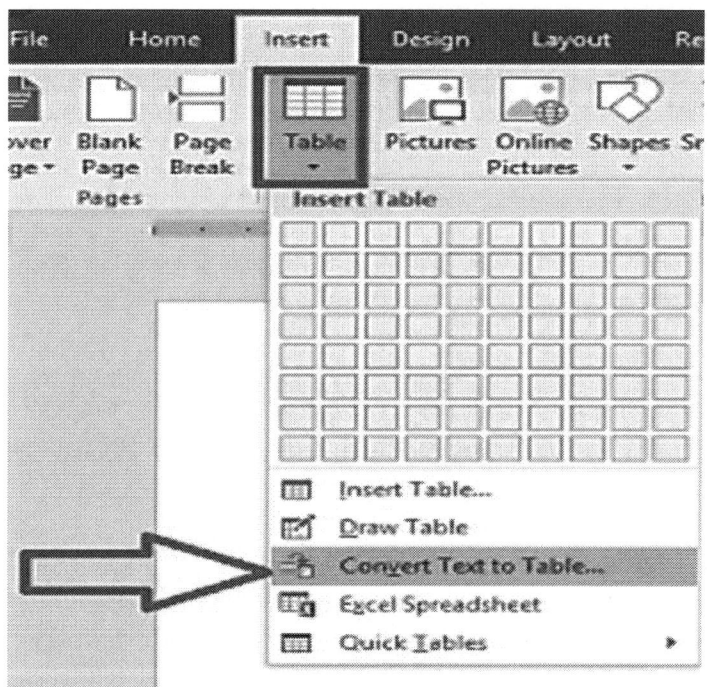

How To Create Bulleted List In Microsoft Word

When constructing a list that stands out from the text, bullet lists come in handy. To make a list using bullets. Place your cursor where you wish the bullet list to appear.

Go to the **home** tab, and on the **paragraph group,** click on the bullet, on the drop-down arrow, click on any bullet that suits you the best. Then type your first list item, after that, press enter and the second line start with the same bullet style. Double-click the enter key to end your bullet list.

To Remove The Bullet And Numbering

Just open the document and go to the home tab, click on the bullet icon and choose none.

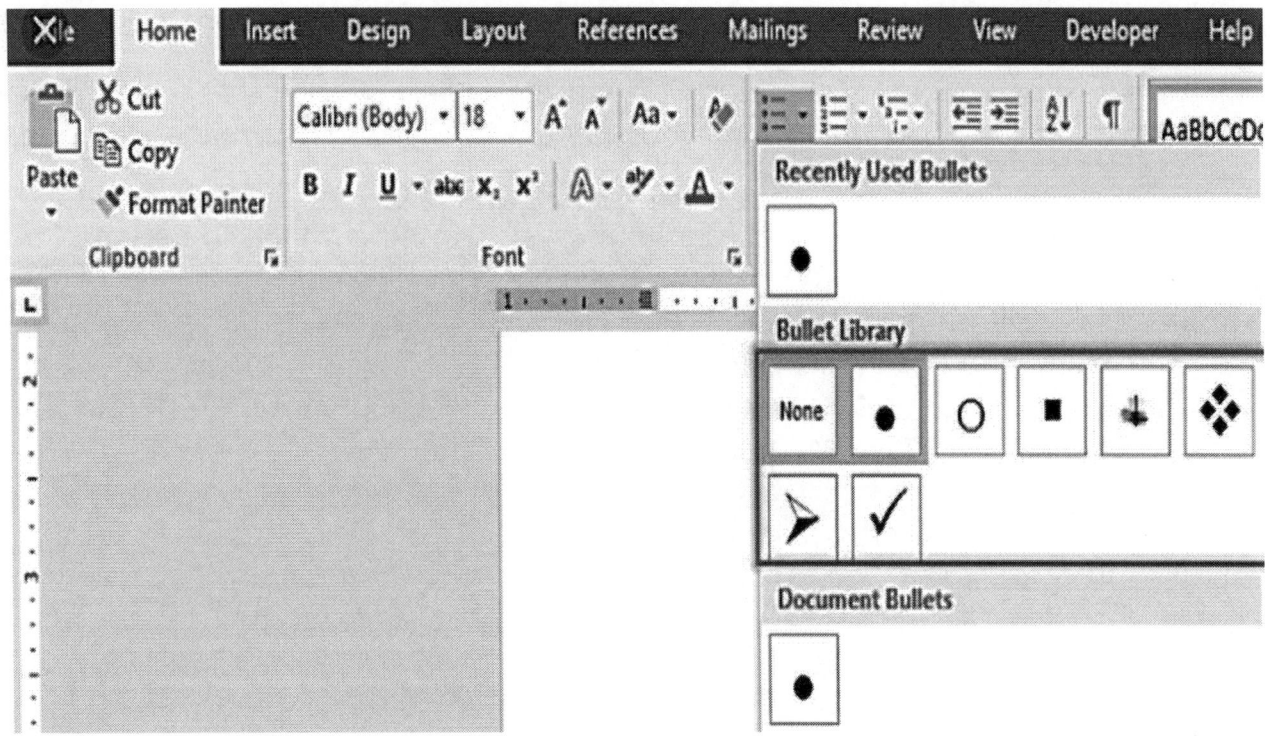

How To Insert Endnote And Footnote On Microsoft 2023

Footnotes are at the bottom of a page while **endnotes** are found at the end of a document. To begin, place your cursor where the superscript number for the footnote should appear. Select the **Reference tab** and select the dialogue box launcher in the footnote group. Select footnote or endnote from the drop-down menu, then select the note's intended location. Other options in the dialogue box, such as number formatting, should be explored. To build your footnote, select insert. After that, type your superscript number, and your cursor will shift to the new spot specified in the footnote and endnote dialogue boxes. Now type your note and double-click the number preceding it to return to the body content's matching superscript number. Insert the next note by placing your cursor where the superscript number for the next note should appear, then selecting Insert footnote or endnote from the footnote and endnote group.

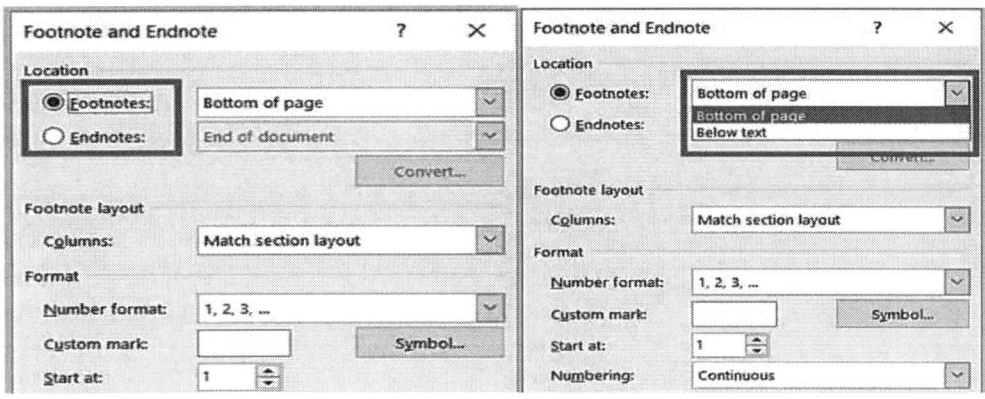

Graphical Works In Microsoft Word 2023

Most of the graphical tools are found on the Insert tab of Microsoft word 2023. Here, you can insert anything into your document including pictures, shapes, text, etc.

To Insert pictures: Place your cursor where you want the image to be inserted and click the Insert tab on the ribbon. The photo tool format tab is one of the commands. It will transport you to areas where you can insert different photos into your work when you click on it. When you've found the image you want, click Insert, and it'll be automatically updated in your document. Use one of the command buttons to select which type of image to add.

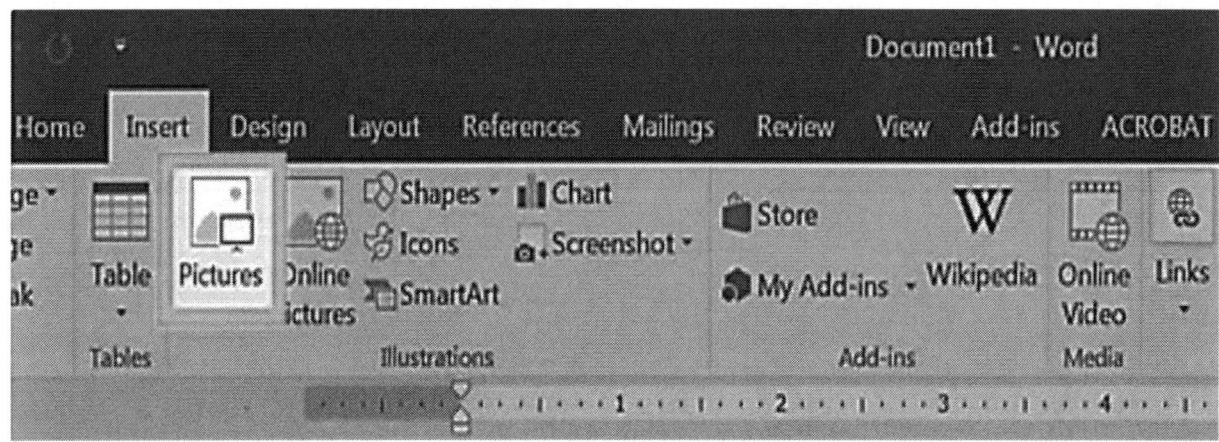

Note: You can also insert online pictures, by clicking on online pictures from the Insert tab. Then copy the image from the web and paste it into your document

- **To Delete an image,** click on the image, select it and click on the delete button.

- **To Copy and Paste an Image;** Select the image you want to copy from another document. Alternatively, press Ctrl + C to copy the image. Then go to the new location where you want to paste that image and click Ctrl + V to paste. Alternatively, right-click the mouse, and options are displayed, choose the paste option to paste the image

How To Insert Shape Into Your Document

You can Insert shapes into your document. Word has a section that contains some common shapes such as circles, squares, arrows, geometric figures, etc. To do this; Click Insert tab and click on the shape button. This menu has lots of shapes that you can choose from. Click on your preferred shape and it is updated into your document.

Note: you can adjust the shape in terms of size or colors. All you have to do is use the drawing tool format tab. This can be seen on the Ribbon. Just select the shapes to effect those changes. You can use the **Shape Fill button t**o set the fill color and you can use the Shape Outline button to set the shape's outline color. You can also adjust the outline thickness (Shape outline button menu) weight and effect (3D, shadow, or any fancy formatting)on the selected shape.

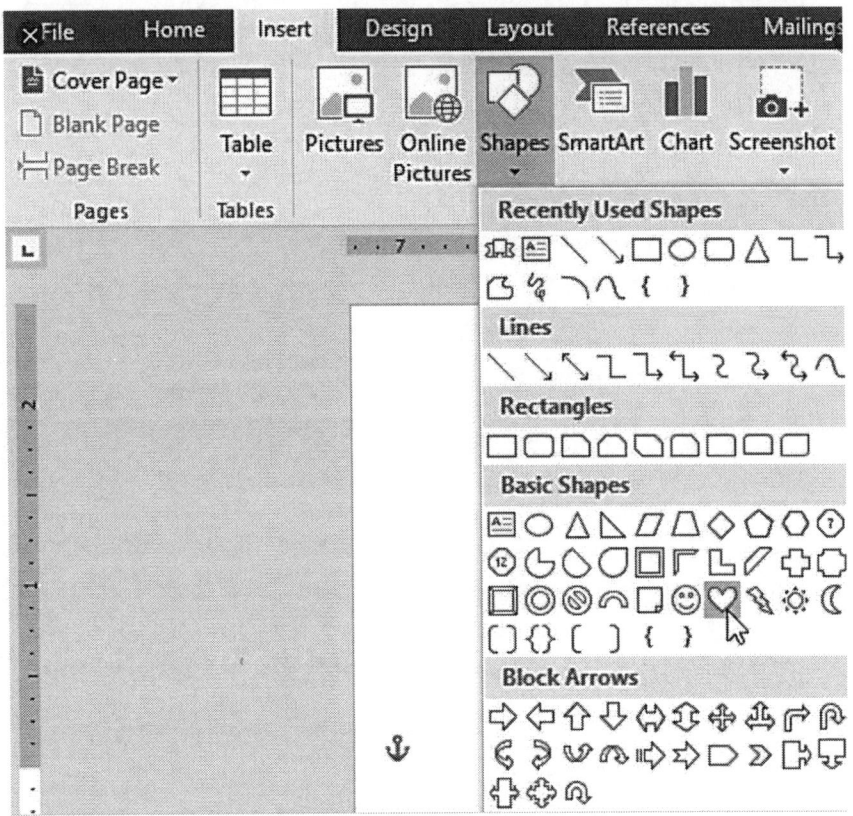

How To Create Picture Layout On Microsoft Word 2023

First of all, select the picture and a new box appears on the selected picture. On the **picture style group,** there is an option for a **picture layou**t. Click on it and then a list of different Layout will be displayed. Click on the one that suits you and resize to the box.

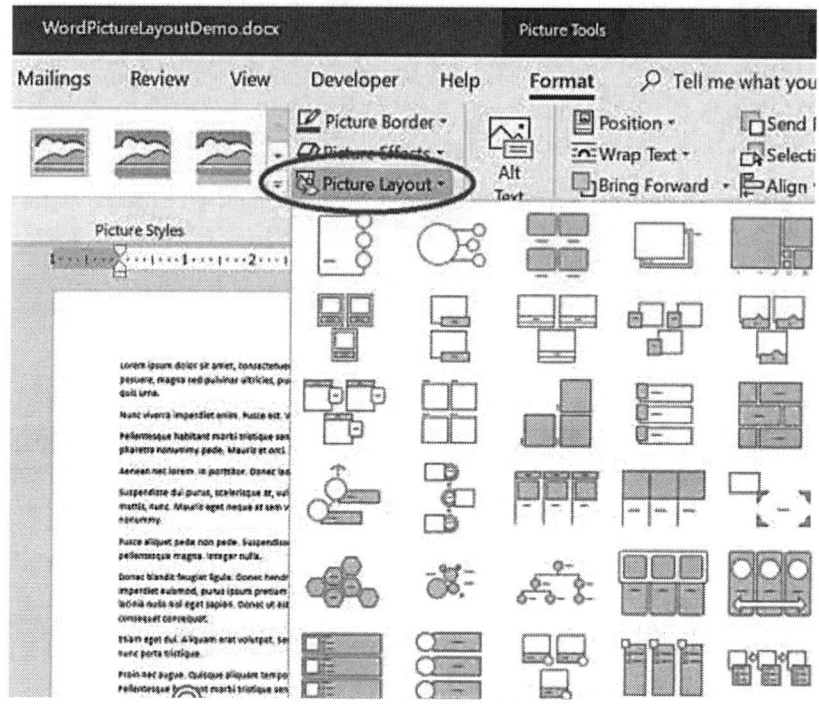

How To Wrap Text Around An Image

It is important to provide a proper layout option to keep all text and images in your document well organized. This layout has 3 general groups. The **Inline** (where the image is inserted into the text and the image acts as a character), **wrapped** (text stays around the image), and **floating (** where the image is seen at the front or behind the text).

To enter an image layout, first select an image, then click the Layout Options button, which displays a list of possible layout options. Inline, square, tight, through, behind the text, top and bottom, front if text, behind the text, wrap text, and so on are some of the alternatives. Click on more selections to see more choices. Choose your favorite option and click OK.

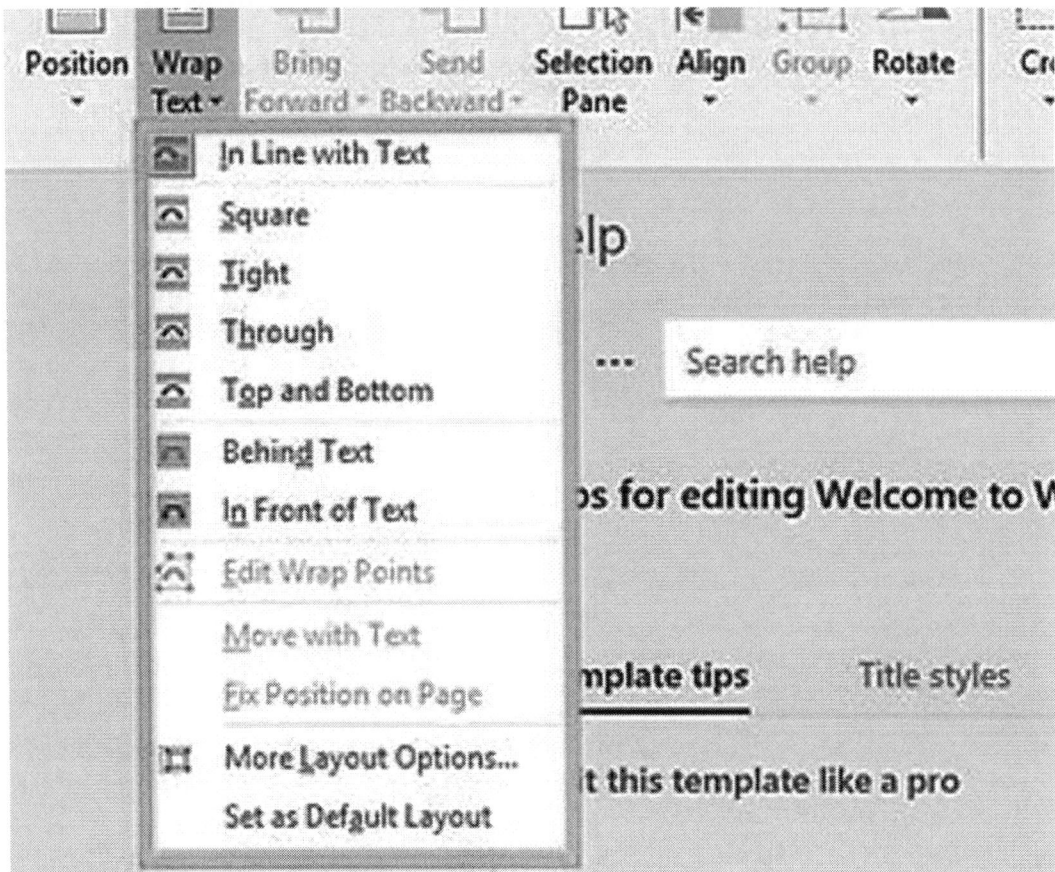

How To Resize An Image

When you click to select an image, eight corner handles display as dots around the image. This is how you scale an image to make it bigger or smaller. To rotate the image, use the top long handle circled on the image with the rotate icon.

How To Crop An Image

To crop an image, click to select the image and on the picture formatting tool in the size group, there is the crop button. Click on the button and press the enter to cut out any part of the image.

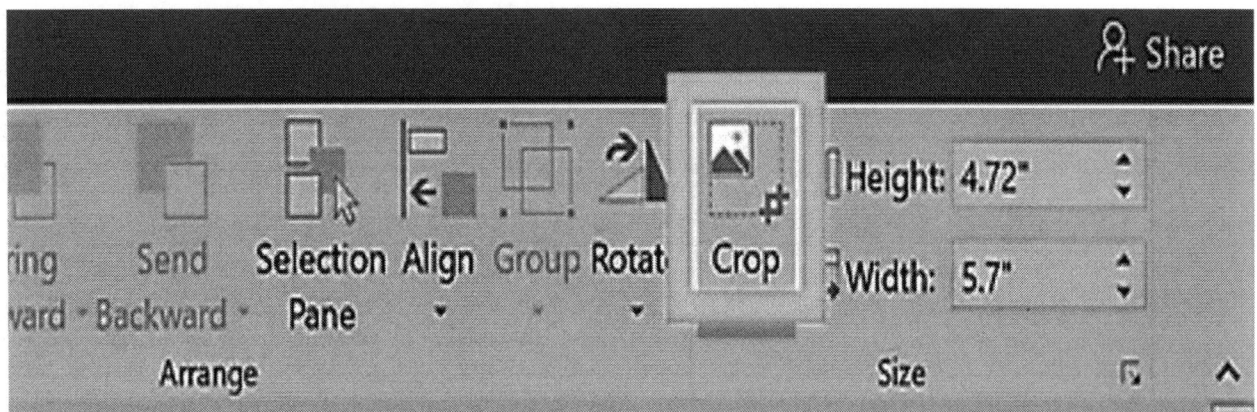

As a way of conclusion, all images can be edited to suit your choice. You can choose to rotate or change the position of the image. This can be achieved with the picture formatting tool.

Chapter 7. Document Management and Collaboration

Saving Your Document

After you've finished producing your document, save it for later use or sharing.

Your document can be saved to your computer, a disk drive, a CD drive, a USB device, or OneDrive. When you save your work in OneDrive, you may access it from any computer that has access to your account.

To save your document for the first time:

1. Click on the **File** tab to go to the backstage of Word.

2. Click **Save As** option in the left-side panel.

3. Select where you want to save your document in the right-side pane.

A dialog box appears.

4. Change the document name to your desired name in the **File Name** box.

5. Select the format in which you want to save your document in the **Save as type** dropdown list.

6. Click **Save**.

You will have to save your work anytime you make changes.

To save your document subsequently,

1. Click on the **Save** icon 🖫 in the quick access toolbar or **Save** tab in the backstage view.

Alternatively,

2. use the shortcut key **Ctrl + s.**

Note: Using the above methods for the document that has never been saved will initiate the **Save as** command.

Your already saved document can also be duplicated with the same or different name and in the same or different location by selecting the **Save As** option in the Word backstage.

Page Setups For Printing

You can get a hard or paper copy of your document by printing.

To print your document:

1. Ensure your computer is connected to the printer.

2. Ensure your printer is loaded with the right size papers.

3. Click the **File** tab to go to the Word backstage.

4. Select **Print** in the left side pane.

Print pane appears by the right-side.

5. Input the number of copies you want directly or with the arrows in the **Copies** box.

6. Select a printer in the **Printer** drop-down if your computer is connected to more than one printer.

7. Under **Settings**, the default settings are shown in each box. To make changes to any, click the drop-down in front of the one you want to change and select your preferred option in the drop-down menu.

- You can print specified page numbers by inputting them in the **Pages** textbox, separated by a comma.

- The paper orientation, page size, and margins appear as you have set them during formatting. You could adjust them here if you desired.

- Click on the **Page Setup** for more page settings.

8. Preview your work in the right section of the **Print** pane to see how it will come out. Make use of the scroll bar to go through the pages.

9. Click the **Print** button.

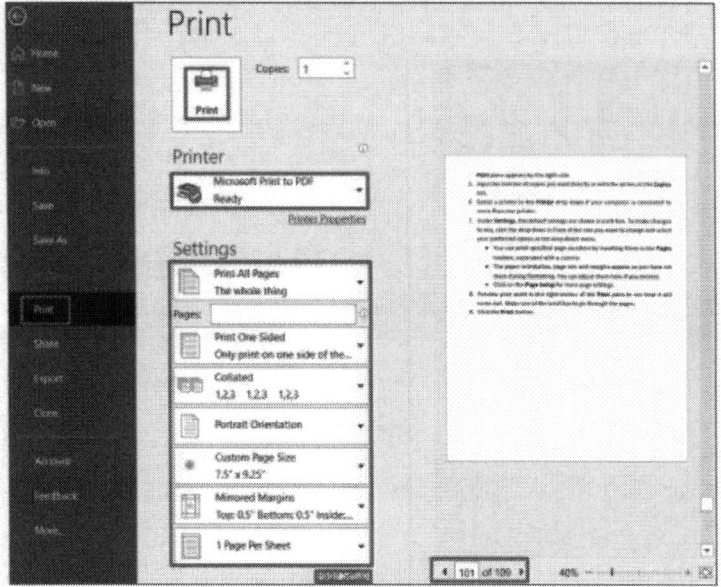

Sharing Document By Email

Your word document can be easily shared directly as an email body or as an attachment to an email address with the **Send to Mail Recipient** command in Word. **Send to Mail Recipient** command is not available in the Word user interface by default and needs to be added. You can preferably add it to the Quick Access Toolbar by customizing it.

To add 'Send to Mail Recipient' to Quick Access Toolbar (QAT):

1. Right-click on the **QAT**.

A dialog box appears.

2. Select **Customize Quick Access Toolbar**.

Word Options dialog box appears.

3. From the **Choose commands from** drop-down list, choose **Commands Not in the Ribbon**.

4. Locate **Send to Mail Recipient** in the list. The list is arranged alphabetically for easy location.

5. Click **Add>>** button.

Word adds it to Customize Quick Access Toolbar.

6. Click **OK,**

and it appears in your Quick Access Toolbar.

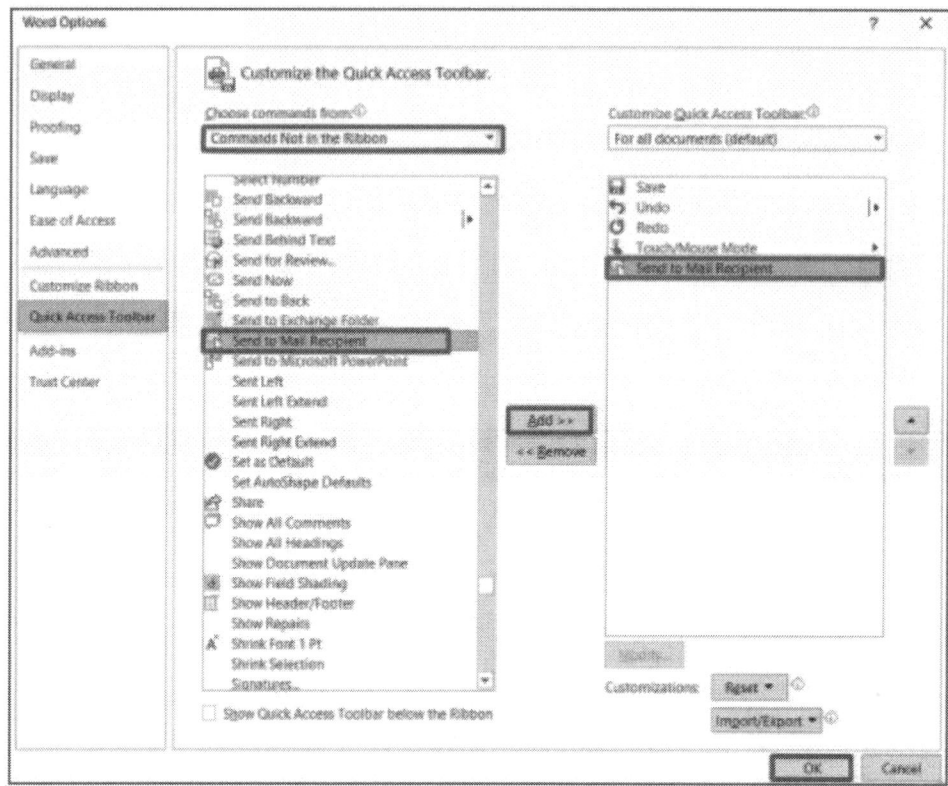

To share your document as an email body:

1. Ensure your computer is connected and sign in to your email account.

2. Click on **Send to Mail Recipient** command in the Quick Access Toolbar.

The mail Composing window appears under the ribbon with your document title already added.

3. Add the recipient's email address and other information as desired. You can also change the title as desired.

4. Ensure you have an internet connection.

5. Click **Send a Copy**.

Word sends your document and closes the composing email window. To close the email window manually, click on the icon in the Quick Access Toolbar.

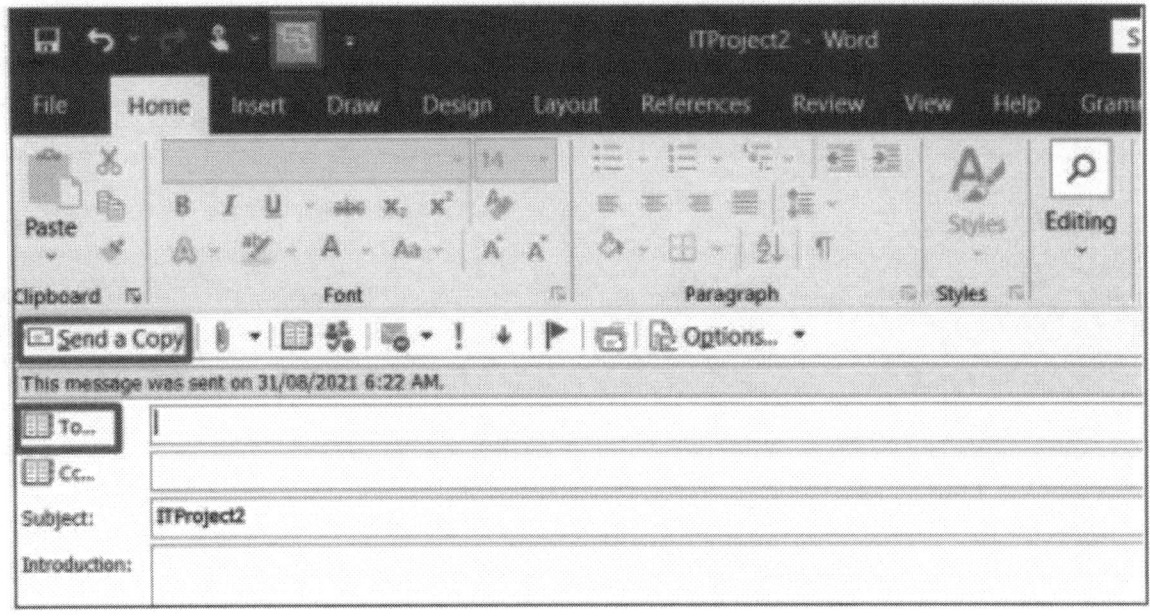

Protecting Your File With Word Security Features

After you've spent time and effort generating your document, you'll need to safeguard it against plagiarism, stealing, inadvertent alteration, and a variety of other security issues.

Word has incredible security capabilities that can help you secure your document depending on how critical it is.

To secure your word document:

1. Go to the Word Backstage by clicking the **File** tab.

2. Click the **Info** tab in the left side pane.

Info pane appears on the right side.

3. Click the **Protect Document** button.

A dialog box appears.

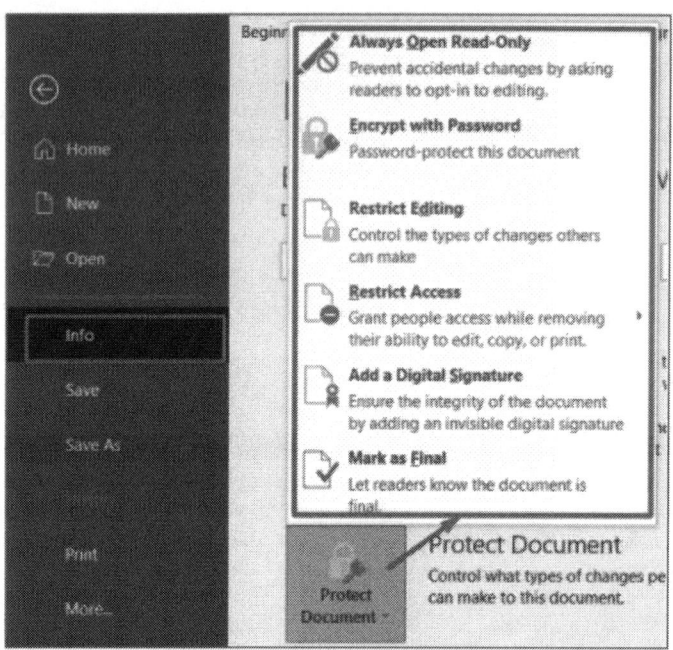

4. Select an option from the list.

- **Mark as Final:** This makes your document read-only (i.e., typing, editing, and proofing capabilities disabled) with a message at the top of the document screen informing the reader that the document is final. However, any reader can still edit and resave the document by clicking the **Edit Anyway** button in the top message. Select this security feature only if you just need to notify the reader that it is the recommended final version of your document or to discourage editing.

- **Add a Digital Signature:** Protecting your document with a digital signature has several benefits, like maintaining proof of document integrity, signer identity, and others. You must purchase a digital signature from a verified Microsoft partner to use it. Selecting this option for the first time will prompt you to where you can get one.

- **Restrict Access:** This allows others to view your document but prevents them from copying, modifying, sharing, or printing it. To help safeguard the document, you'll need to connect to the Information Right Management (IRM) server. If you choose this option, you will be prompted to connect and guided through the procedure.

- **Restrict Editing:** This is a flexible way of securing your document from anyhow editing and gives control over the type of editing that the allowed people can do. Selecting this option opens a pane on the right side of the document to set formatting restrictions, editing restrictions, and **start enforcement**.

- **Encrypt with Password:** Adding a password to your document is a powerful kind of security, and you can only offer the password to people you want to have access to it. Without the password, no one will be able to open, let alone change, your document. When you choose this option, Word will prompt you to enter a password and confirm it.

- **Always Open Read-Only:** This feature prevents your document from accidental editing by always opening it as read-only. A dialog box appears each time you want to open it, notifying you that the document will be opened as read-only. Press **Yes** to continue and **No** if there is a need to make changes.

5. Follow all the prompts based on your choice and press ok.

6. Close your document for the security setting to take effect.

Closing Your Word Document

To close your document after you are done:

- Click the **X** button at the top-right corner of the Word window.

Or

- Go to the **File** tab and select the **Close** option in the left-side pane.

Or

- Use the shortcuts keys, **Ctrl + F4** or **Ctrl + W.**

Microsoft word closes or notifies you if you try to close your document without saving it.

Recovering Unsaved Document

It can happen that you mistakenly close your document without saving your last changes. The good news is that Word has an **autosave** feature that allows you to recover your file with the last unsaved changes.

To recover your unsaved documents:

1. Go to the backstage view by clicking on the **File** tab.

2. Click the **Open** tab.

Open pane appears.

3. Click the **Recover Unsaved Documents** button at the bottom of the recently opened document list.

The location dialog box appears with the list of unsaved documents.

4. Select the likely document. You can check the date to know the likely document.

5. Click the **Open** button.

The document opens.

6. Save the document accordingly.

Alternatively,

1. Go to the backstage view by clicking on the **File** tab.

2. Click the **Info** tab.

Info pane opens.

3. Select **Manage Document** dropdown.

4. Click the **Recover Unsaved Documents** menu that appears.

The location dialog box appears with the list of unsaved documents.

5. Follow **steps 4-6** above.

Opening Saved Document

You can open your document from the Word application or directly from your device.

To open an existing document from Word:

> 1. Go to the backstage view by clicking on the **File** tab.
>
> 2. Click the **Open** tab.

Open pane appears.

> 3. Select the location of your document.

Open dialog box appears.

> 4. Select the folder or your document. You can scroll down the left side list of locations on your device to locate your document.
>
> 5. Click **Open**.

Alternatively, if you recently opened your document or pinned it to Word, it will be available in the **Recent** or **Pinned** list in the backstage **Home** panel, and you can click on it to open it.

If you often use or work on your document, it will be better to pin it in Word.

To pin your document to word:

> 1. Locate the document in the recent list.
>
> 2. Move your cursor over the document.
>
> 3. Click the pin icon in front of the file.

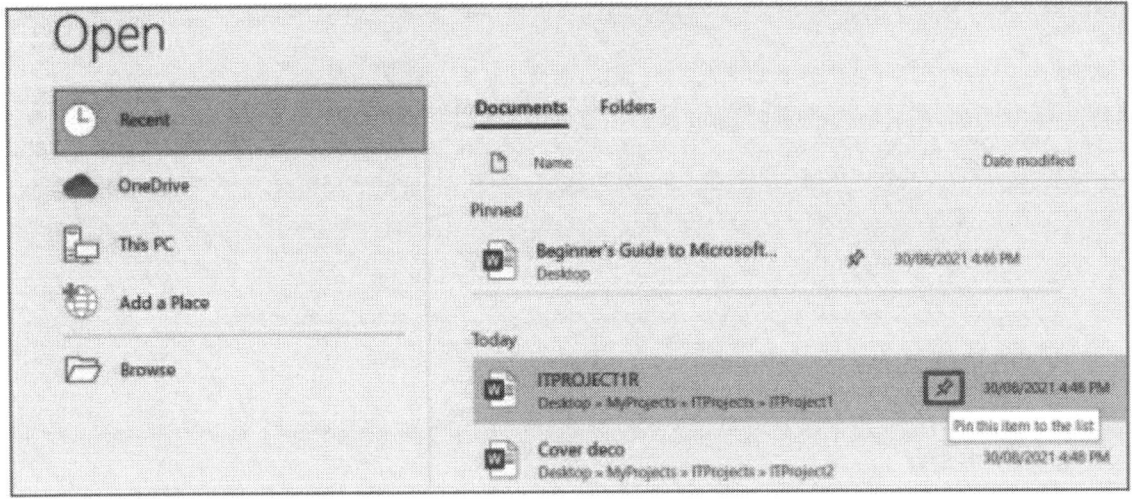

To open an existing document from your device:

1. Ensure you have the Word application installed on your computer.

2. Locate your Word document on your device.

3. Double-click to open it if it has a Word icon, if not, right-click on the file.

Select **open with** from the menu that appears and select **Word**.

Chapter 8. Streamlining Your Workflow

Working with Keyboard shortcut commands can reduce your stress, save your time and increase your productivity to a considerable extent. Below are the top shortcut commands you can use to work smartly in Word.

SN	Shortcuts	Functions	
1.	Ctrl + A	4. To select all the content of your document	
2.	Ctrl + B	5. To bold the highlighted contents	
3.	Ctrl + C	6. To copy highlighted text	
4.	Ctrl + D	7. To open a Font dialog box	
5.	Ctrl + E	8. To center align the selected content	
6.	Ctrl + F	9. To open the **Find Navigation** pane	
7.	Ctrl + G	10. To open the **Go To** dialogue window	
8.	Ctrl + H	To open the **Replace** dialog box.	
9.	Ctrl + I	11. To italicize highlighted contents	
10.	Ctrl + J	12. To justify align selected content	
11.	Ctrl + K	13. To open the **Insert Hyperlink** dialog box.	

12.	Ctrl + L	14. To left-align selected content	
13.	Ctrl + M	15. To increase the Indent	
14.	Ctrl + N	To create a new blank document	
15.	Ctrl + O	To open an already saved document	
16.	Ctrl + P	To go to **the Print** tab in the backstage view	
17.	Ctrl + Q	To reset selected paragraph	
18.	Ctrl + R	To right-align selected content	
19.	Ctrl + S	To save your current document	
20.	Ctrl + T	To increase the Hanging indent of the selected paragraph.	
21.	Ctrl + U	To underline the selected text.	
22.	Ctrl + V	To paste what you copied last.	
	Ctrl + W	To close your document	

No.	Shortcut	Description	
23.			
24.	Ctrl + X	To cut selected content	
25.	Ctrl + Y	To redo the last action, you undo.	
26.	Ctrl + Z	To undo your last action	
27.	Shift +Ctrl +A	To apply the All caps command	
28.	Shift +Ctrl +C	To copy Format	
29.	Shift +Ctrl +D	To double underline selected text	
30.	Shift +Ctrl +G	To open the Word count dialog box	
31.	Shift +Ctrl +J	To distribute the letters of the selected text evenly	
32.	Shift +Ctrl +K	To apply the Small-cap command	
33.	Shift +Ctrl +L	To apply bullet listing.	
	Shift +Ctrl +M	To decrease Indent	

34.			
35.	**Shift +Ctrl +N**	To apply Normal Style of the **Style** group.	
36.	**Shift +Ctrl +O**	To open the research pane	
37.	**Shift +Ctrl +P**	To open the Font dialog box	
38.	**Shift +Ctrl +Q**	To set the Font to symbol.	
39.	**Shift +Ctrl +T**	To decrease Hanging Indent.	
40.	**Shift +Ctrl +V**	To open the Paste Format window.	
41.	**Shift +Ctrl +W**	To underline each word of the selected content.	
42.	**Esc**	To cancel an active command	
43.	**F1**	To open Microsoft Word **Help**	
44.	**Ctrl + Alt + V**	To display the **Paste Special** dialog box	
	Ctrl + Shift + F	To open the Fonts tab of the **Format Cells** dialog box.	

45.			

Chapter 9: Keyboard shortcuts in Word

Windows

Frequently used shortcuts

To do this	Press
Open a document.	Ctrl+O
Create a new document.	Ctrl+N
Save the document.	Ctrl+S
Close the document.	Ctrl+W
Cut the selected content to the Clipboard.	Ctrl+X
Copy the selected content to the Clipboard.	Ctrl+C
Paste the contents of the Clipboard.	Ctrl+V
Select all document content.	Ctrl+A
Apply bold formatting to text.	Ctrl+B
Apply italic formatting to text.	Ctrl+I
Apply underline formatting to text.	Ctrl+U
Decrease the font size by 1 point.	Ctrl+Left bracket ([)
Increase the font size by 1 point.	Ctrl+Right bracket (])
Center the text.	Ctrl+E
Align the text to the left.	Ctrl+L
Align the text to the right.	Ctrl+R
Cancel a command.	Esc
Undo the previous action.	Ctrl+Z
Redo the previous action, if possible.	Ctrl+Y
Adjust the zoom magnification.	Alt+W, Q, then use the Tab key in the **Zoom** dialog box to go to the value you want.
Split the document window.	Ctrl+Alt+S
Remove the document window split.	Alt+Shift+C or Ctrl+Alt+S

Use the Access Keys for ribbon tabs

To do this	Press
Move to the **Tell Me** or **Search** field on the Ribbon to search for assistance or Help content.	Alt+Q, then enter the search term.
Open the **File** page to use Backstage view.	Alt+F
Open the **Home** tab to use common formatting commands, paragraph styles, and the Find tool.	Alt+H
Open the **Insert** tab to insert tables, pictures and shapes, headers, or text boxes.	Alt+N
Open the **Design** tab to use themes, colors, and effects, such as page borders.	Alt+G
Open the **Layout** tab to work with page margins, page orientation, indentation, and spacing.	Alt+P
Open the **References** tab to add a table of contents, footnotes, or a table of citations.	Alt+S
Open the **Mailings** tab to manage Mail Merge tasks and to work with envelopes and labels.	Alt+M
Open the **Review** tab to use Spell Check, set proofing languages, and to track and review changes to your document.	Alt+R
Open the **View** tab to choose a document view or mode, such as Read Mode or Outline view. You can also set the zoom magnification and manage multiple document windows.	Alt+W

Work in the ribbon with the keyboard

To do this	Press
Select the active tab on the ribbon and activate the access keys.	Alt or F10. To move to a different tab, use access keys or the arrow keys.
Move the focus to commands on the ribbon.	Tab key or Shift+Tab
Move between command groupings on the ribbon.	Ctrl+Left or Right arrow key
Move among the items on the ribbon.	Arrow keys
Show the tooltip for the ribbon element currently in focus.	Ctrl+Shift+F10
Activate the selected button.	Spacebar or Enter

To do this	Press
Open the list for the selected command.	Down arrow key
Open the menu for the selected button.	Alt+Down arrow key
When a menu or submenu is open, move to the next command.	Down arrow key
Expand or collapse the ribbon.	Ctrl+F1
Open the context menu.	Shift+F10 Or, on a Windows keyboard, the Windows Menu key (between the right Alt and right Ctrl keys)
Move to the submenu when a main menu is open or selected.	Left arrow key

Navigate the document

To do this	Press
Move the cursor one word to the left.	Ctrl+Left arrow key
Move the cursor one word to the right.	Ctrl+Right arrow key
Move the cursor up by one paragraph.	Ctrl+Up arrow key
Move the cursor down by one paragraph.	Ctrl+Down arrow key
Move the cursor to the end of the current line.	End
Move the cursor to the beginning the current line.	Home
Move the cursor to the top of the screen.	Ctrl+Alt+Page up
Move the cursor to the bottom of the screen.	Ctrl+Alt+Page down
Move the cursor by scrolling the document view up by one screen.	Page up
Move the cursor by scrolling the document view down by one screen.	Page down
Move the cursor to the top of the next page.	Ctrl+Page down
Move the cursor to the top of the previous page.	Ctrl+Page up
Move the cursor to the end of the document.	Ctrl+End
Move the cursor to the beginning of the document.	Ctrl+Home
Move the cursor to the location of the previous revision.	Shift+F5

To do this	Press
Move the cursor to the location of the last revision made before the document was last closed.	Shift+F5, immediately after opening the document.
Cycle through floating shapes, such as text boxes or images.	Ctrl+Alt+5, and then the Tab key repeatedly
Exit the floating shape navigation and return to the normal navigation.	Esc
Display the **Navigation** task pane, to search within the document content.	Ctrl+F
Display the **Go To** dialog box, to navigate to a specific page, bookmark, footnote, table, comment, graphic, or other location.	Ctrl+G
Cycle through the locations of the four previous changes made to the document.	Ctrl+Alt+Z

Navigate the document using the browse options in Word 2007 and 2010

To do this	Press
Open the list of browse options to define the type of object to browse by.	Ctrl+Alt+Home
Move to the previous object of the defined type.	Ctrl+Page up
Move to the next object of the defined type.	Ctrl+Page down

Preview and print documents

To do this	Press
Print the document.	Ctrl+P
Switch to print preview.	Ctrl+Alt+I
Move around the preview page when zoomed in.	Arrow keys
Move by one preview page when zoomed out.	Page up or Page down
Move to the first preview page when zoomed out.	Ctrl+Home
Move to the last preview page when zoomed out.	Ctrl+End

Select text and graphics

To do this	Press
Select text.	Shift+Arrow keys
Select the word to the left.	Ctrl+Shift+Left arrow key
Select the word to the right.	Ctrl+Shift+Right arrow key
Select from the current position to the beginning of the current line.	Shift+Home
Select from the current position to the end of the current line.	Shift+End
Select from the current position to the beginning of the current paragraph.	Ctrl+Shift+Up arrow key
Select from the current position to the end of the current paragraph.	Ctrl+Shift+Down arrow key
Select from the current position to the top of the screen.	Shift+Page up
Select from the current position to the bottom of the screen.	Shift+Page down
Select from the current position to the beginning of the document.	Ctrl+Shift+Home
Select from the current position to the end of the document.	Ctrl+Shift+End
Select from the current position to the bottom of the window.	Ctrl+Alt+Shift+Page down
Select all document content.	Ctrl+A

Extend a selection

To do this	Press
Start extending the selection.	F8 In the extend selection mode, clicking a location in the document extends the current selection to that location.
Select the nearest character to the left or right.	F8, Left or Right arrow key

To do this	Press
Expand the selection.	F8 repeatedly to expand the selection to the entire word, sentence, paragraph, section, and document.
Reduce the selection.	Shift+F8
Select a vertical block of text.	Ctrl+Shift+F8, then press the arrow keys
Stop extending the selection.	Esc

Edit text and graphics

To do this	Press
Delete one word to the left.	Ctrl+Backspace
Delete one word to the right.	Ctrl+Delete
Open the **Clipboard** task pane and enable the Office Clipboard, which allows you to copy and paste content between Microsoft 365 apps.	Alt+H, F, O
Cut the selected content to the Clipboard.	Ctrl+X
Copy the selected content to the Clipboard.	Ctrl+C
Paste the contents of the Clipboard.	Ctrl+V
Move the selected content to a specific location.	F2, move the cursor to the destination, and then press Enter.
Copy the selected content to a specific location.	Shift+F2, move the cursor to the destination, and then press Enter.
Define an AutoText block with the selected content.	Alt+F3
Insert an AutoText block.	The first few characters of the AutoText block, and then press Enter when the ScreenTip appears.
Cut the selected content to the Spike.	Ctrl+F3
Paste the contents of the Spike.	Ctrl+Shift+F3
Copy the selected formatting.	Ctrl+Shift+C
Paste the selected formatting.	Ctrl+Shift+V
Copy the header or footer used in the previous section of the document.	Alt+Shift+R

To do this	Press
Display the **Replace** dialog box, to find and replace text, specific formatting, or special items.	Ctrl+H
Display the **Object** dialog box, to insert a file object into the document.	Alt+N, J, J
Insert a SmartArt graphic.	Alt+N, M
Insert a WordArt graphic.	Alt+N, W

Align and format paragraphs

To do this	Press
Center the paragraph.	Ctrl+E
Justify the paragraph.	Ctrl+J
Align the paragraph to the left.	Ctrl+L
Align the paragraph to the right.	Ctrl+R
Indent the paragraph.	Ctrl+M
Remove a paragraph indent.	Ctrl+Shift+M
Create a hanging indent.	Ctrl+T
Remove a hanging indent.	Ctrl+Shift+T
Remove paragraph formatting.	Ctrl+Q
Apply single spacing to the paragraph.	Ctrl+1
Apply double spacing to the paragraph.	Ctrl+2
Apply 1.5-line spacing to the paragraph.	Ctrl+5
Add or remove space before the paragraph.	Ctrl+0 (zero)
Enable AutoFormat.	Ctrl+Alt+K
Apply the **Normal** style.	Ctrl+Shift+N
Apply the **Heading 1** style.	Ctrl+Alt+1
Apply the **Heading 2** style.	Ctrl+Alt+2
Apply the **Heading 3** style.	Ctrl+Alt+3
Display the **Apply Styles** task pane.	Ctrl+Shift+S
Display the **Styles** task pane.	Ctrl+Alt+Shift+S

Format characters

To do this	Press
Display the **Font** dialog box.	Ctrl+D or Ctrl+Shift+F
Increase the font size.	Ctrl+Shift+Right angle bracket (>)
Decrease the font size.	Ctrl+Shift+Left angle bracket (<)
Increase the font size by 1 point.	Ctrl+Right bracket (])
Decrease the font size by 1 point.	Ctrl+Left bracket ([)
Switch the text between upper case, lower case, and title case.	Shift+F3
Change the text to all upper case.	Ctrl+Shift+A
Hide the selected text.	Ctrl+Shift+H
Apply bold formatting.	Ctrl+B
Add a bulleted list.	Ctrl+Shift+L
Apply underline formatting.	Ctrl+U
Apply underline formatting to the words, but not the spaces.	Ctrl+Shift+W
Apply double-underline formatting.	Ctrl+Shift+D
Apply italic formatting.	Ctrl+I
Apply small caps formatting.	Ctrl+Shift+K
Apply subscript formatting.	Ctrl+Equal sign (=)
Apply superscript formatting.	Ctrl+Shift+Plus sign (+)
Remove manual character formatting.	Ctrl+Spacebar
Change the selected text to the Symbol font.	Ctrl+Shift+Q

Manage text formatting

To do this	Press
Display all nonprinting characters.	Ctrl+Shift+8 (do not use the numeric keypad)
Display the **Reveal Formatting** task pane.	Shift+F1

Insert special characters

To do this	Press
Insert a line break.	Shift+Enter
Insert a page break.	Ctrl+Enter
Insert a column break.	Ctrl+Shift+Enter
Insert an em dash (—).	Ctrl+Alt+Minus sign (on the numeric keypad)
Insert an en dash (–).	Ctrl+Minus sign (on the numeric keypad)
Insert an optional hyphen.	Ctrl+Hyphen (-)
Insert a nonbreaking hyphen.	Ctrl+Shift+Hyphen (-)
Insert a nonbreaking space.	Ctrl+Shift+Spacebar
Insert a copyright symbol (©).	Ctrl+Alt+C
Insert a registered trademark symbol (®).	Ctrl+Alt+R
Insert a trademark symbol (™).	Ctrl+Alt+T
Insert an ellipsis (...)	Ctrl+Alt+Period (.)
Insert the Unicode character for the specified Unicode (hexadecimal) character code. For example, to insert the euro currency symbol ( ), type 20AC, and then hold down Alt and press X. **Tip:** To find out the Unicode character code for a selected character, press Alt+X.	The character code, then press Alt+X
Insert the ANSI character for the specified ANSI (decimal) character code. For example, to insert the euro currency symbol, hold down Alt and press 0128 on the numeric keypad.	Alt+the character code (on the numeric keypad)

Work with web content

To do this	Press
Insert a hyperlink.	Ctrl+K
Go back one page.	Alt+Left arrow key
Go forward one page.	Alt+Right arrow key
Refresh the page.	F9

Move around in a table

To do this	Press
Move to the next cell in the row and select its content.	Tab key
Move to the previous cell in the row and select its content.	Shift+Tab
Move to the first cell in the row.	Alt+Home
Move to the last cell in the row.	Alt+End
Move to the first cell in the column.	Alt+Page up
Move to the last cell in the column.	Alt+Page down
Move to the previous row.	Up arrow key
Move to the next row.	Down arrow key
Move one row up.	Alt+Shift+Up arrow key
Move one row down.	Alt+Shift+Down arrow key

Select table content

To do this	Press
Select the content in the next cell.	Tab key
Select the content in the previous cell.	Shift+Tab
Extend a selection to adjacent cells.	Shift+Arrow keys
Select a column.	Select the top or bottom cell of the column, and then press Shift+Up or Down arrow key
Select a row.	Select the first or last cell in the row, and then press Shift+Alt+End or Home.

To do this	Press
Select the whole table.	Alt+5 on the numeric keypad, with Num Lock switched off

Insert paragraphs and tab characters in a table

To do this	Press
Insert a new paragraph in a cell.	Enter
Insert a tab character in a cell.	Ctrl+Tab

Review a document

To do this	Press
Insert a comment.	Ctrl+Alt+M
Turn change tracking on or off.	Ctrl+Shift+E
Close the **Reviewing Pane**.	Alt+Shift+C

Work with references, citations, and indexing

To do this	Press
Mark a table of contents entry.	Alt+Shift+O
Mark a table of authorities entry (citation).	Alt+Shift+I
Choose citation options.	Alt+Shift+F12, Spacebar
Mark an index entry.	Alt+Shift+X
Insert a footnote.	Ctrl+Alt+F
Insert an endnote.	Ctrl+Alt+D
Go to the next footnote.	Alt+Shift+Right angle bracket (>)
Go to the previous footnote.	Alt+Shift+Left angle bracket (<)

Perform a mail merge

To do this	Press
Preview the mail merge.	Alt+Shift+K
Merge a document.	Alt+Shift+N
Print the merged document.	Alt+Shift+M

To do this	Press
Edit a mail-merge data document.	Alt+Shift+E
Insert a merge field.	Alt+Shift+F

Work with fields

To do this	Press
Insert a DATE field.	Alt+Shift+D
Insert a LISTNUM field.	Ctrl+Alt+L
Insert a PAGE field.	Alt+Shift+P
Insert a TIME field.	Alt+Shift+T
Insert an empty field.	Ctrl+F9
Update the linked information in a Word source document.	Ctrl+Shift+F7
Update the selected fields.	F9
Unlink a field.	Ctrl+Shift+F9
Switch between a selected field code and its result.	Shift+F9
Switch between all field codes and their results.	Alt+F9
Run GOTOBUTTON or MACROBUTTON from a field displaying field results.	Alt+Shift+F9
Go to the next field.	F11
Go to the previous field.	Shift+F11
Lock a field.	Ctrl+F11
Unlock a field.	Ctrl+Shift+F11

Set the proofing language

To do this	Press
Display the **Language** dialog box to set the proofing language.	Alt+R, U, L
Set default languages.	Alt+R, L

Insert international characters

To insert this	Press
à, è, ì, ò, ù,	Ctrl+Grave accent (`), the letter

To insert this	Press
À, È, Ì, Ò, Ù	
á, é, í, ó, ú, ý Á, É, Í, Ó, Ú, Ý	Ctrl+Single quotation mark ('), the letter
â, ê, î, ô, û Â, Ê, Î, Ô, Û	Ctrl+Shift+Caret (^), the letter
ã, ñ, õ Ã, Ñ, Õ	Ctrl+Shift+Tilde (~), the letter
ä, ë, ï, ö, ü, ÿ, Ä, Ë, Ï, Ö, Ü, Ÿ	Ctrl+Shift+Colon (:), the letter
å, Å	Ctrl+Shift+At sign (@), a or A
æ, Æ	Ctrl+Shift+Ampersand (&), a or A
œ, Œ	Ctrl+Shift+Ampersand (&), o or O
ç, Ç	Ctrl+Comma (,), c or C
ð, Ð	Ctrl+Single quotation mark ('), d or D
ø, Ø	Ctrl+Forward slash (/), o or O
¿	Ctrl+Alt+Shift+Question mark (?)
¡	Ctrl+Alt+Shift+Exclamation point (!)
ß	Ctrl+Shift+Ampersand (&), s

Use Input Method Editors for East Asian languages

To do this	Press
Switch to the Japanese Input Method Editor (IME) for a 101-key keyboard, if available.	Alt+Tilde (~)
Switch to the Korean Input Method Editor (IME) for a 101-key keyboard, if available.	Right Alt
Switch to the Chinese Input Method Editor (IME) for a 101-key keyboard, if available.	Ctrl+Spacebar

Switch the document view

To do this	Press
Switch to the **Read Mode** view.	Alt+W, F

To do this	Press
In Word 2007 and 2010, this is called **Full Screen Reading** view.	
Switch to the **Print Layout** view.	Ctrl+Alt+P
Switch to the **Outline** view.	Ctrl+Alt+O
Switch to the **Draft** view.	Ctrl+Alt+N

Outline a document

To do this	Press
Promote a paragraph.	Alt+Shift+Left arrow key
Demote a paragraph.	Alt+Shift+Right arrow key
Demote the paragraph to body text.	Ctrl+Shift+N
Move the selected paragraphs up.	Alt+Shift+Up arrow key
Move the selected paragraphs down.	Alt+Shift+Down arrow key
Expand the text under a heading.	Alt+Shift+Plus sign (+)
Collapse the text under a heading.	Alt+Shift+Minus sign (-)
Expand or collapse all text or headings.	Alt+Shift+A
Hide or display the character formatting.	Forward slash (/) (on the numeric keypad)
Switch between showing the first line of body text and showing all body text.	Alt+Shift+L
Show all headings with the **Heading 1** style.	Alt+Shift+1
Show all headings with the specified heading level.	Alt+Shift+Heading level number
Insert a tab character.	Ctrl+Tab

Move through the document in Read Mode

To do this	Press
Move to the beginning of the document.	Home
Move to the end of the document.	End
Go to a specific page.	Type the page number, then press Enter
Exit Read Mode.	Esc

CONCLUSION

Harnessing the Full Potential of Microsoft Word 2024

As we reach the end of the "Microsoft Word Quick Start 2024 Guide," it's important to reflect on the journey we've embarked upon together. This guide was designed not just to introduce you to the features of Microsoft Word 2024, but to empower you to use them effectively in your personal and professional endeavors.

A Journey of Discovery and Mastery

Throughout the chapters, we've explored the expansive capabilities of Microsoft Word 2024. Beginning with the basics of obtaining and installing the software, we ventured through the intricacies of its interface, delving into the depths of document creation, editing techniques, and the art of enhancing document presentation. The journey through organizing complex content, document management, collaboration, workflow streamlining, and mastering keyboard shortcuts provided a comprehensive understanding of what makes Word 2024 an indispensable tool.

The Evolving Landscape of Word Processing

Microsoft Word 2024, as showcased in this guide, is a testament to the evolution of word processing. It combines the foundational elements of traditional word processing with innovative features that address the needs of modern users. From its enhanced user interface to its advanced collaboration tools, Word 2024 is more than just a program; it's a gateway to effective and efficient digital communication.

Embracing the Power of Effective Communication

The skills and knowledge you've gained from this guide are tools for effective communication. Whether drafting a simple letter, compiling a detailed report, or crafting a creative document, Word 2024 offers the resources to convey your message with clarity and impact. The guide's emphasis on customization, accessibility, and user-friendliness ensures that Word 2024 is adaptable to your unique requirements.

The Future of Digital Literacy

As digital literacy becomes increasingly crucial in both professional and personal spheres, mastering a tool like Microsoft Word 2024 positions you at the forefront of this digital revolution. The competencies you've developed through this guide are not just technical skills; they're a part of a broader set of digital literacy skills that are vital in today's world.

A Commitment to Continuous Learning

The world of technology is ever-changing, and so is Microsoft Word. This guide serves as a foundation, but the journey doesn't end here. Continuous learning and adaptation are key to staying proficient with Word 2024 and future versions. Stay curious, explore new updates, and keep refining your skills.

The Essence of Productivity and Creativity

In the "Microsoft Word Quick Start 2024 Guide", we emphasized not just the functional aspects of Microsoft Word 2024, but also its role in fostering productivity and creativity. Every chapter, every section was carefully crafted to help you unlock your potential in both these spheres. As you move forward, remember that Word 2024 is a canvas for your ideas, a tool that can transform thoughts into tangible, impactful documents.

Productivity: Streamlining Your Workflow

One of the core themes of this guide was enhancing productivity. Microsoft Word 2024, with its advanced features and intuitive interface, is designed to streamline your workflow. The guide walked you through shortcuts, customization tips, and automation features that reduce time spent on repetitive tasks, allowing you to focus on the content that matters. Remember, efficiency in Word 2024 is not just about speed; it's about making the process smoother and more enjoyable.

Creativity: Unleashing Your Potential

Creativity in document design and presentation is another cornerstone of Word 2024. This guide introduced you to a plethora of tools for adding a creative touch to your documents. From inserting and editing images to customizing layouts and styles, Word 2024 is equipped to bring a creative flair to your work. As you continue to explore these features, you'll find that your documents can become not just a medium of information, but a reflection of your creativity and attention to detail.

The Role of Collaboration and Connectivity

In a world where collaboration is key, Microsoft Word 2024 stands as a vital tool for teamwork and connectivity. This guide highlighted how Word 2024 breaks down geographical barriers, enabling real-time collaboration, sharing, and communication. As you move forward, leverage these collaborative tools to work effectively with colleagues, classmates, and friends, enhancing the quality of your joint projects and fostering a spirit of teamwork.

Embracing a Global Workspace

Word 2024's cloud integration and collaboration features make it a global workspace. Whether you are working on a personal project or a professional assignment, the ability to access, edit, and share your documents from anywhere in the world is a powerful asset. This guide aimed to make you comfortable and proficient with these global capabilities, preparing you for a world where remote work and digital collaboration are the norms.

Continuing Your Learning Journey

While this guide provides a comprehensive overview of Microsoft Word 2024, it is important to view it as a starting point rather than an end. Technology, and specifically software like Microsoft Word, is constantly evolving. Staying updated with new features, exploring additional resources, and practicing your skills are crucial for maintaining proficiency.

Resources for Ongoing Learning

Consider exploring online forums, tutorials, and official updates from Microsoft to stay abreast of the latest advancements in Word 2024. Joining user groups or online communities can also provide valuable insights and tips from fellow users.

Final Reflections

As we conclude the "Microsoft Word Quick Start 2024 Guide", it's important to acknowledge the journey you've embarked upon. From a beginner, or perhaps an intermediate user, to a proficient and confident navigator of Microsoft Word 2024, you've equipped yourself with skills that will serve you well in various aspects of your digital life.

Remember, the true power of Microsoft Word 2024 lies in how you apply it. Whether it's in crafting compelling stories, presenting data in engaging ways, or collaborating on projects that span continents, Word 2024 is your ally. Embrace the possibilities, explore the potentials, and most importantly, keep writing your story, one word at a time.

Final Thoughts

In closing, the "Microsoft Word Quick Start 2024 Guide" is more than just a guidebook - it's a companion in your journey of mastering Microsoft Word 2024. The knowledge and skills you've acquired are stepping stones to greater efficiency, creativity, and effectiveness in your digital documentation endeavors. As you continue to explore and utilize the powerful features of Word 2024, remember that the power of this tool lies in how you use it to transform your ideas into reality.

Thank you for choosing this guide as your companion on this journey. May your experiences with Microsoft Word 2024 be fruitful and rewarding. Here's to a future of empowered writing and seamless digital communication!

Printed in Great Britain
by Amazon

50040000R00071